Global Education Inc.

Do private and philanthropic solutions to the problems of education signal the end of state education in its 'welfare' form?

Education policy is being reformed and re-worked on a global scale. Policies are flowing and converging to produce a singular vision of 'best practice' based on the methods and tenets of the 'neo-liberal imaginary'. Philanthropy, business and the governments are coming together in new networks and sites of policy outside of the framework of the nation state. This book is a first step in recording, mapping and making sense of the most important aspects of these new relations and dynamics of policy.

Using the approach of 'policy sociology' and the methods of social network analysis *Global Education Inc.* explores the policy activities of edu-businesses, neo-liberal advocacy networks and policy entrepreneurs, and of social enterprises and 'new' philanthropy. It also addresses the ways in which education and education policy itself are now being exported and bought and sold as profitable commodities and how entrenched problems of educational development and educational quality and access are now being addressed through 'market solutions'. That is, by the involvement of private providers in the delivery of educational services, both independently and on behalf of the state.

Universities, schools and education services are being acquired as assets by private equity companies. Private storefront schools are being set-up by local entrepreneurs and through franchising arrangements, funded through microloans. School chains funded by philanthropy and run by multi-national edu-businesses are being harnessed to the attempts of developing societies in an attempt to achieve their Millennium Development Goals and provide mass access to basic education. Curriculum materials and pedagogy software and policy ideas such as inspections, leadership, school choice and account-ability are being retailed by western 'knowledge companies' and consultants across the globe. This book argues that these new forms of policy and policy-making require new concepts and methods of policy analysis, with chapters including:

- Networks, neo-liberalism and policy mobilities
- 'New' philanthropy, social capitalism and education policy
- Policy as profit: selling and exporting policy
- Money, meaning and policy connections

Global Education Inc. is a crucial book that will be of great interest to students of social and education policy and social and education policy analysts and researchers.

Stephen J. Ball is Karl Mannheim Professor of Sociology of Education at the Institute of Education, University of London, UK.

Global Education Inc.

New policy networks and the neo-liberal imaginary

Stephen J. Ball

Routledge
Taylor & Francis Group

LONDON AND NEW YORK

First published 2012
by Routledge
2 Park Square, Milton Park, Abingdon, Oxon OX14 4RN

Simultaneously published in the USA and Canada
by Routledge
711 Third Avenue, New York, NY 10017

Routledge is an imprint of the Taylor & Francis Group, an informa business

British Library Cataloguing in Publication Data
A catalogue record for this book is available from the British Library

Library of Congress Cataloging in Publication Data
Ball, Stephen J.
Global education inc. : policy networks and edu-business / Stephen J. Ball.
p. cm.
1. Privatization in education. 2. Education and globalization.
3. Neoliberalism. I. Title.
LB2806.36.B353 2012
379.1'11–dc23   2011039500

ISBN: 978-0-415-68409-5 (hbk)
ISBN: 978-0-415-68410-1 (pbk)
ISBN: 978-0-203-80330-1 (ebk)

Typeset in Garamond
by Taylor & Francis books

Printed and bound in Great Britain by
TJ International Ltd, Padstow, Cornwall

... to be free is not merely to cast off one's chains, but to live in a way that respects and enhances the freedom of others. The true test of our devotion to freedom is just beginning.

Nelson Mandela, *The Long Walk to Freedom*, p. 751
(Abacus, London, 1994)

To Brian Davies and Tony Knight
Two good men and true

Contents

Figures and boxes

Figures

Boxes

Acknowledgements

This book would not have got written without a lot of help from a lot of people. In particular and especially Trinidad Ball, and Antonio Olmedo, Geetha Nambissan and Carolina Junemann. It draws in part on an ESRC funded research project, ESRC RES-000-22-2682.

Chapter 3 is based on joint research and writing done with Geetha Nambissan at JNU, Dehli (Nambissan and Ball, 2010) and in places draws heavily on searches done by Geetha; direct quotation from the paper is indicated in the text. Chapter 4 also draws on a lot of background searches done by Ono Olmedo, and other work we are doing together; he also put together several of the network diagrams in the book and read and commented on the text, with great patience. Carolina Junemann also read and commented on the text for me, constructed diagrams and completed the formatting. Diego Santori did searches and made comments. The peculiarities that remain are mine.

Chapter 5 is partly based on Ball 2009 and Chapter 6 on Ball 2011a and Ball 2011b.

I am also grateful to Michael Apple and the Havens Center, University of Wisconsin-Madison for their hospitality and the opportunity to speak about my work and to Kalervo Gulson and Colin Mills. Anna Clarkson was enthusiastic and patient.

Foreword

(Not) reading this book

It is very difficult to direct the way in which people read your book, and impossible to control the meaning they make of the text, but here I shall at least try to influence the way in which you engage with this book.

Four things

First, the book is in part a workbook. It is an attempt to develop a method of policy analysis fitted to the current context of global education policy. A lot of things are being tried out for size. Some of the ideas or analyses you may think do not work or could be done differently. That is fine! I hope you will decide to take on some of the approaches outlined and take them further. I have realised in writing the book and doing the background research that there is an enormous gap in the research field of education policy. Despite all of the talk about globalization this and globalization that, and a few nods and gestures towards new forms of governance, most education policy analysis is still locked into a nation-state, policy-as-government paradigm. Most such analysis is looking at only some of the places in which policy is now being done. We lack tools and perspectives suited to the task of a more cosmopolitan sociology of policy. Beck describes a 'cosmopolitan sociology' – as a necessary condition for grasping the dynamics of an increasingly cosmopolitan reality: 'Cosmopolitanisation is a non-linear, dialectical process in which the universal and particular, the similar and the dissimilar, the global and the local are to be conceived, not as cultural polarities, but as interconnected and reciprocally interpenetrating principles' (Beck, 2006, pp. 72–73). That is what is attempted in this book. Beck goes on to say:

> How can social and political theory be opened up, theoretically, empirically as well as methodologically and normatively, to historically new, entangled modernities which threaten their own foundations? How can it account for the fundamental fragility and mutability of societal dynamics (of unintended side-effects, domination and power), shaped, as they are, by the globalization of capital and risks at the beginning of the

21st century? What theoretical and methodological problems arise and how can they be addressed in empirical research? So what has to be done?

(Beck and Grande, 2010, p. 409)

Second, the examples given and used are partial, superficial and very time-sensitive. The processes of change in policy and provision which I seek to describe are incredibly fast moving. Much of the substance of the book will be out of date by the time it is published. That is the nature of the beast. Again, though, I hope that the analysis work that is offered will have a half-life beyond the specific instances.

Third, and this is difficult. I do not take up a simple or obvious position in relation to neo-liberalism, although it is fashionable to do so. Some people are perplexed by this but what I am trying to do here is to provide tools and methods for thinking about neo-liberalism rather than telling you what I think you should think about it. Further, there are some things that I report in the book that make me uncomfortable or angry, there are other things I am unsure or ambivalent about. The neo-liberalism I describe is often mundane and certainly not of a piece. Certainly I do not find it easy to condemn as a matter of course programmes and initiatives which offer access to education to children who otherwise have no opportunity to attend school. Also, as I say several times below, we as yet know little about 'what is really going on'. Again this is a plea for more research so that we might be a little clearer about what we think. We are faced with deciding in 'conditions of undecidability' (Derrida, 1996 'remarks'), as well as being positioned in all of this, being complicit, imbricated and compromised. Neo-liberalism is not just 'out there' (Peck and Tickell, 2003). Having said that I do not pretend that the book is neutral.

Fourth, and more prosaically, there is a lot of 'stuff' in the book, and a lot of this 'stuff' comes from internet searches. I am trying to be grounded and specific about the phenomena and processes I am addressing. I would encourage you to check out some of the websites and do some searches of your own. The 'data' is there for you to explore, it is not tucked away in my computer files. You can test the adequacy of my accounts and my analysis, you can find further examples, and look at more recent developments.

So in reading this book I hope you will appreciate its limits, and what more needs to be done; take up and try out some of the ideas; do more searches; and decide for yourself what you think and whether you want to get angry and get involved – in one way or another!

1 Networks, neo-liberalism and policy mobilities

There is no simple narrative or structure to this book, it is in part a 'workbook', the application and development of a method, but it also interweaves a set of analytic and substantive themes which recur and develop through the chapters.

Introduction

The book is a sequel to *Education plc* (S. J. Ball, 2007), which was an empirical and conceptual account of the participation of business in public sector education in England. *Education plc* sought to map and categorise the range of types of such private sector involvement, to identify the different sorts of companies and organisations 'interested' in such involvement, and to consider how this involvement was changing the policy process and policy communities and was related to changes in the education state – that is, the emergence of a new kind of state. This book takes that work further and sets it more broadly within what I will call 'global education policy' (see also Rizvi & Lingard, 2010). The book will also engage with some of the main tenets of recent writing and research on governance and changes in the form and modalities of the state and draw on some ongoing developments in policy analysis method.

Here then I will offer an account of contemporary trends in education reform and public sector governance, starting from England but moving out to describe and analyse new global developments in education policy, with examples from a wide range of settings and policy developments. In particular the book will focus on the increasing role of business, social enterprise and philanthropy in education service delivery and education policy, and the concomitant emergence of new forms of 'network' governance, or what I shall later in the book refer to as 'heterarchies'. These are dynamic and very immediate changes that have a national and global significance in relation to education policy, education reforms, democracy, social opportunity and equity, and the meaning and practice of education.

The book examines the advocacy and dissemination of 'private' and social enterprise solutions to the 'problems' of state education, using examples from Latin America, the USA, India, Africa, South-East Asia and England, and explores the ways in which policy 'moves' between these locations and around the globe, and certain trends towards what Jessop (2002, p. 202) calls the 'denationalization of the state'. I will argue substantively that significant changes are taking place in how policy and public services get 'done', nationally and globally – set within a 'variable coincidence of different boundaries, borders or frontiers of action and the changing primacy of different scales' (Jessop, 2002, p. 49). In relation to education I will suggest that the sum of these changes indicates the beginning of the end of state education in its 'welfare' form(s). A set of new, blurred relationships and 'interests' within policy and within state education will be outlined. I will also consider whether the changes and reforms described represent the triumph of 'the neo-liberal imaginary', that is:

> Globalisation as experienced over the past thirty years or so has been neoliberal globalisation, an ideology which promotes markets over the state and regulation and individual advancement/self-interest over the collective good and common well being. We have seen a new individualism, with individuals now being deemed responsible for their own 'self-capitalising' over their lifetimes. Common good and social protection concerns have been given less focus and the market valued over the state, with enhanced market or private sector involvement in the workings of the state.
>
> (B. Lingard, 2009, p. 18)

The book is not an abstract or theoretical discussion of neo-liberalism, nor is it a rhetorical critique of neo-liberalism. Rather it focuses on the *how* of neo-liberalism. How it is promoted. How it is 'done'. How it 'works'. It gets inside some of what Wendy Larner calls the 'micro-spaces' of neo-liberalism (Larner & Le Heron, 2002) and some of its mundane practices – everyday, ordinary neo-liberalism. It looks inside the business heartlands of neo-liberalism – 'start-ups', edupreneurs, knowledge companies, acquisitions and mergers, private equity, multinationalism, and vertical and horizontal integration. That is, the new financescapes of global edu-business and their mysterious, rapid, and difficult landscape (Appadurai, 1996). It also examines the advocacy and dissemination of 'private' and philanthropic solutions to the 'problems' of state education. All of this is intended as a response to both Wendy Larner's (2003) challenge that 'we need a more careful tracing of the intellectual, policy, and practitioner networks that under-pin the global expansion of neo-liberal ideas, and their subsequent manifestation in government policies and programmes' (p. 510) and Peck and Tickell's (2003, p. 229) call for more detailed conceptualisations and 'descriptions of the circulatory systems that connect and interpenetrate "local" policy regimes'.

What is neo-liberalism?

I want to make clear from the outset that I use the term neo-liberal here with some trepidation. It is one of those terms that is used so widely and so loosely that it is in danger of becoming meaningless. What I mean here by neo-liberalism is expressed very nicely by Shamir (2008, p. 3). Neo-liberalism, he says:

> Is treated neither as a concrete economic doctrine nor as a definite set of political projects. Rather, I treat neoliberalism as a complex, often incoherent, unstable and even contradictory set of practices that are organized around a certain imagination of the 'market' as a basis for 'the universalisation of market-based social relations, with the corresponding penetration in almost every single aspect of our lives of the discourse and/or practice of commodification, capital-accumulation and profit-making'
>
> (Carvalho and Rodrigues, 2006, citing Wood 1997).

Such a view of neo-liberalism recognises both the material and the social relations involved, that is both the neo-Marxist focus on the 'economisation' of social life and the 'creation' of new opportunities for profit, what Ong (2007) calls neo-liberalism with a big 'N', and a Foucauldian analytics of governmentality, and particularly the governing of populations through the production of 'willing', 'self-governing', entrepreneurial selves, what Ong calls neo-liberalism with a small 'n' – which is reconfiguring relationships between governing and the governed, power and knowledge, and sovereignty and territoriality (Ong, 2007, p. 4). Analysing neo-liberalism in these ways involves being both 'post' and 'neo' as Michael Apple puts it; it is a 'balancing act' (Apple, 1995). In the examples deployed in this book there is a complex interplay of material forces, relations and interests, and a set of 'practices, relationships and forms of organization that are discursively constituted as economic' (Clarke, 2008, p. 137). Neo-liberalism is about both money and minds, and as I shall go on to argue is a nexus of common interest between various forms of contemporary capital and the contemporary state.

Peck and Tickell (2002) identify three interrelated and uneven phases, waves or processes of neo-liberalism; they are 'proto' neo-liberalism, 'roll-back' neo-liberalism and 'roll-out' neo-liberalism. 'Proto neo-liberalism' is the intellectual project, shaped by Hayek and Friedman and other economic and libertarian theorists, that was critical in the discursive construction of a political and economic crisis around the Keynesian welfare state and an 'alternative' to it. With intellectual roots traceable back to Adam Smith and David Ricardo, the catalyst for the revival of liberal economic state theory was Frederick Hayek's excoriating analysis of collectivism in *The Road to Serfdom* (1944). 'Roll-back neo-liberalism' refers to 'the active destruction or discreditation of Keynesian-welfarist and social-collectivist institutions (broadly defined)' (p. 37). The third neo-liberal wave, 'roll-out neo-liberalism', refers to 'the purposeful construction and consolidation of neo-liberalized state forms, modes of governance, and regulatory relations' (Peck & Tickell, 2002, p. 398) in order to stabilise or further entrench neo-liberalism through the introduction of new institutions, policies and governmentalities. Peck and Tickell also point to the need to consider neo-liberalism's adaptability, its 'ongoing dynamic of discursive adjustment, policy learning, and institutional reflexivity' (2002, p. 392).

As soon as we take neo-liberalism seriously it becomes clear that education policy analysis can no longer be limited to within the boundaries of the nation state, what Jessop, Brenner et al. (2008, p. 391) call *methodological territorialism*, and indeed some of the ongoing developments in global policy raise questions about whether more and more states are losing the ability to control their education systems – denationalisation. Education policy is being 'done' in new locations, on different scales, by new actors and organisations. For example:

> Imagine a room filled with the most innovative, action-oriented, and socially responsible leaders in the world. The Clinton Global Initiative's Annual Meeting brings together heads of state, government and business leaders, scholars, and NGO directors. Participants analyze pressing global challenges, discuss the most effective solutions, and build lasting partnerships that enable them to create positive social change. The 2010 Annual Meeting will take place in New York from September 21–23.
> (http://www.clintonglobalinitiative.org/ourmeetings/default.
> asp? Section=OurMeetings&PageTitle=Our%20Meetings,
> accessed 25 August 2010)

These new scales and locations, forms of participation and relationship require new methods and concepts and new research sensibilities. Researchers must also adapt, reflect and learn.

Policy network analysis

Substantively, the book draws upon a series of research studies of philanthropy, privatisation and policy reform in education and cognate fields. These have been funded by the ESRC.[1] The research was carried out between 2004 and 2011. This research has involved three sets of activities; extensive and exhaustive internet searches around particular edu-businesses, corporate and family philanthropies, philanthropists and philanthropically funded programmes – material 'captured' in this way includes webpages and documents, but also videos, powerpoints, facebook pages and blogs and tweets; interviews with some key edu-business people, 'new' philanthropists and philanthropic foundations interested and involved in education and attendance at some related meetings and events; and the use of these searches and interviews to construct 'policy networks' which have been subject to detailed analysis. Together these constitute something that might be called a 'method' of 'network ethnography' (Howard, 2002), a mapping of the form and content of policy relations in a particular field, a variation of what Bevir and Rhodes (2006) present as 'ethnographic analyses of governance in action'. Howard (2002, p. 550) makes the point that: 'Whereas social network analysis renders an overarching sketch of interaction, it will fail to capture detail on incommensurate yet meaningful relationships' – network ethnography aims to go some way in remedying this failure and the use of new forms of virtual and electronic communication, as above, offers a broader and richer access to the 'social' in social networks than has been the case using just terrestrial data.

In more general terms this 'method' is set within a broad set of epistemological and ontological shifts across political science, sociology and social geography which involve a lessening of interest in social structures, and an increasing emphasis on flows and mobilities (of people, capital and ideas e.g. 'policies in motion' (Peck, 2003)) – what Urry (2003, p. 157) calls the 'mobility turn'. That is, a focus on the 'spatializing' of social relations, on travel and other forms of movement and other transnational interactions and forms of sociality. All of this is of course attendant upon the overwhelming interest in recent years in the processes of 'globalization'. Again, as with neo-liberalism, the focus on *mobilities* takes into account large-scale economic and political changes on the one hand, and cultural changes and changes in identity and subjectivity on the other[2] and what Larner (2003, p. 511) calls the 'apparently mundane practices' through which the global is produced. *The network* is a key trope and analytic device within this refocusing of attention as a kind of connective tissue which joins up and provides *some* durability to these distant and fleeting forms of social interaction – 'circulatory systems that connect and interpenetrate' the local (Peck, 2003, p. 229). As Urry (2003, p. 170) puts it very simply: 'Social life at least for many in the "west" and "north" is increasingly networked'. However, I also take heed of Jessop, Brenner et al.'s (2008, p. 391–92) warning against what they call *network-centrism*, that is a 'one-sided focus on horizontal, rhizomatic, topological and transversal interconnections of networks, frictionless spaces of flows, and accelerating mobilities' – the construction of a 'flat ontology'. Rather, they urge the need for 'historically specific geographies of social relations' (p. 392) and the exploration of 'contextual and historical variation'. The detailed account of neo-liberal schooling developments in India (Chapter 3) is one of several attempts in this book to avoid such 'flatness'.

Policy networks are one type of the new 'social', involving particular kinds of social relationships, flows and movements. They constitute policy communities, usually based upon shared conceptions of social problems and their solutions; as Agranoff (2003, p. 28) puts it, 'networks provide venues for collaborative solutions' and 'mobilise innovations', although they sometimes contain 'strange bedfellows' (as we shall see). Through them new voices are given space within policy talk. New narratives about what counts as a 'good' policy are articulated and validated (see Ball, 2007). People move across and within such communities, and there are new kinds of policy and governance careers which can be constructed within them. In some cases, as we shall see, there are 'real' self-consciously constructed and maintained networks (e.g. Atlas, Chapter 2). These policy networks work through forms of 'contact'; however, the nature of the relations between members (as represented by the arrows in the figures) is not the same in every case. Participations are multifaceted and forms of relationship are diverse: individual actors may be involved in networks in a variety of different ways, e.g. sponsorship, contracting, and so on. Dicken, Kelly & Yeung (2001) assert that the task of network methodology 'must be to identify the actors in these networks, their power and capacities, and the ways through which they exercise their power through association within networks of relationships' (p. 93).

Network analysis and network governance

Let me say a little more about social network analysis and policy networks. There is a degree of misleading clarity about the concept of networks, particularly as used in the governance literature. It is either used very abstractly to describe general changes in the form of government or deployed to refer to a very wide variety of real and practical social relationships. Furthermore, some of the writing on networks is normative and the distinction between prescription and analysis is sometimes blurred. Indeed, Besussi (2006, p. 2) suggests that 'nowhere is to be found a common understanding of what policy networks are and how they operate. Little agreement exists even on whether policy networks are to be considered as a metaphor, a method or a proper theory with explanatory power'. In what follows *network* is deployed in two different but related ways.

1. As noted already, network is a method, an analytic technique for looking at the structure of policy communities and their social relationships. It works to capture and describe *some aspects* of these relationships, that is some of the more *visible* aspects of these relationships. However, neither the analytic nor the descriptive aspects of the method are without difficulties. Some of these difficulties have been well rehearsed in the social network analysis literature but I will return to and draw attention to some that are relevant here in a moment.

2. Network is also a conceptual device in this account. It is used to represent a set of 'real' changes in the forms of governance of education, both nationally and globally. By 'examining networks we are looking at the institutionalization of power relations' (Marsh & Smith, 2000, p. 6). This is what is often called *network governance*, although the term is used somewhat

loosely and diversely. In general terms, what network governance refers to is the treatment of seemingly intractable public policy problems – 'wicked issues' that 'defy efforts to delineate their boundaries and to identify their causes' (Rittel and Webber 1973, p. 167 in Williams 2002, p. 104) – through forms of managerial, organisational and entrepreneurial response 'around collaboration, partnership and networking' (Williams, 2002). That is, a 'shared' problem-solving process which offers opportunities to participate in governance work to a wider variety of actors than previously. 'The promise of policy networks and of the mode of governance they represent is to produce more effective and legitimate policies, without resting upon the authority and limitations of a single representative political body' (Besussi, 2006, p. 18). Governments are increasingly 'catalyzing all sectors – public, private and voluntary – into action to solve their community's problems' (Osborne & Gaebler, 1992). It is also suggested that catalysing brings a greater degree of flexibility and adjustment to the complexity of existing conditions (see Chapter 4) and other social and economic actors can provide an environment for consensus building and therefore limit the resistance to innovation (Marin & Mayntz, 1991). However, this shift also involves forms of experimentation and ad hocery (see Parker, 2007) and policy failures. In all of this, Shamir (2008, p. 6) argues, 'governments relinquish some of their privileged authoritative positions'. The move to use forms of network governance in some areas of state activity may involve a loss of power in some parts of the state, at the same time as there are gains in other parts. If the gains are bigger than the losses (to use power very crudely) then the state may overall have greater powers than before. However, the state is also acquiring new powers and forms of power. It is important that we do not underestimate the powers of the state but also important that we do not in the abstract overestimate them, nor treat the state as an undifferentiated whole. In slightly stronger terms Rhodes argues that network governance 'refers to self-organising, inter-organizational networks characterized by interdependence, resource-exchange, rules of the game, and significant autonomy from the state' (Rhodes, 1997, p. 15). We can see this in the ways that public services are increasingly delivered through a mix of 'strategic alliances, joint working arrangements, networks, partnerships and many other forms of collaboration across sectoral and organizational boundaries' (Williams, 2002, p. 103) and in the increase in 'relations involving mutuality and interdependence as opposed to hierarchy and independence' (Peterson, 2003, p. 1). In general terms this is the move towards a 'polycentric state' and 'a shift in the centre of gravity around which policy cycles move' (Jessop, 1998, p. 32), although many of the accounts of network governance omit entirely the role of the private sector in these movements and interdependences.

Some writers argue that these network-based forms of coordination are displacing hierarchy and markets and developing as the dominant mode of governance and social organisation (Kooiman, 1993; Pierre, 2000; Pierre &

Peters, 2000; Rhodes, 1997)[3] and go on to relate the changes involved to a move to more democratic forms of governance (Sorenson & Tofting, 2007) while other writers suggest that network governance creates a 'democratic deficit' as the processes of policy and governance become more dispersed and more opaque (March & Olsen, 1989; Skelcher, 1998). That is, not only do policy networks blur the boundaries between state and society but they also expose the policy-making process to particularistic power games. The 'territory of influence' (Mackenzie & Lucio, 2005) over policy is expanded and at the same time the spaces of policy are diversified and dissociated. As a result, as these new sites within the contexts of influence and text production (Ball, 1994) proliferate, there is a concomitant increase in the opacity of policy-making. Within their functioning it is unclear what may have been said to whom, where, with what effect and in exchange for what (see Cohen, 2004). Policy is being privatized in a number of senses (see Chapter 5).

The use of network as an analytic device for researching and describing and visualising governance relationships has its problems. One very basic issue raised by Goodwin (2009) is whether the use of the device actually constructs the outcome, that 'if you look for networks you will find them'. There is some truth to that but the response is to be able to demonstrate the effects of networks, or the work networks do in terms of policy processes and governance. Having said that, the distribution of power and capabilities within policy networks is not easy to 'measure' or represent. It is sometimes difficult to map empirically 'the structured relationships of power' (Goodwin, 2009, p. 682) within policy networks. How do we access and then 'measure' or calculate differential resources and capabilities embedded within the asymmetries in power relations? How do we relate these to the use of power and the different interests and goals of participants? A focus on specific events or crises may be one way forward. I believe that we have no well-worked research methods for addressing these tasks. Among other difficulties, almost by definition, network relations are opaque, consisting in good part of informal social exchanges, negotiations and compromises which go on 'behind the scenes'. How are these to be mapped and characterised? There are also concomitant conceptual and empirical problems arising from the (in)stability and short-term existence of some networks and network relations. Again almost by definition, network forms of governance are not fixed, and may contain some fleeting, fragile and experimental components. 'Networks are informal and fluid, with shifting membership and ambiguous relationships and accountabilities' (Newman, 2001, p. 108). How do we capture changes in participation, capabilities and asymmetries over time? This is both an analytical and representational problem. The representational problem arises in as much as network diagrams are very inadequate and misleading devices for representing networks. Put most simply, but most pointedly, the question is, both in the construction and representation of network diagrams – what do the arrows mean? What sorts of relationships and/or exchanges do they stand for? Are they equivalent? What is the strength of these relationships? What is the direction of flow? How do the relationships and their strengths change over time? There are some forms of quantitative analysis of social networks which have sought to 'measure' networks in a literal sense – their degree of integration or interconnectedness, and their boundaries, the identification of nodes or hegemons or boundary spanners or holes. However, there is a mismatch between what can be measured and what, from the point of view of policy sociology, is interesting and significant. I shall address some of these problems in the various analyses which follow and I hope to point to some ways forward for the policy network method – but I cannot promise simple or clear solutions.

Policy networks and global education policy

Given the differences and difficulties that I have adumbrated above I will begin with a set of assertions which I draw from my research, of which I shall then hope to convince the reader through the presentation and discussion of various global education policy networks in the rest of the book.

So, I contend that policy networks do constitute a new form of governance, albeit not in a single and coherent form, and bring into play in the policy process new sources of authority and indeed a 'market of authorities' (Shamir, 2008, p. 10). Within all of this the modalities and contents of education policy and service delivery *are* changing (what Burch (2009) calls 'the field effects' of new forms of participation); nationally the educational state *is* more congested; new relationships and forms of relationships *are* being established in and in relation to policy, that is to say, there *is* a new mix within the matrix of governance involving 'complex relations of reciprocal interdependence' (Jessop, 2002, p. 52); the boundaries between state, economy and civil society *are* being blurred; there are new voices within policy conversations and new conduits through which policy discourses enter policy thinking; and *there is* a proliferation of policy networks nationally and globally made up of 'operationally autonomous' but 'structurally coupled' organisations (Jessop, 2002, p. 202). *Generally, at the global level there is* also for national governments, especially those of small and fragile states, a reduction in their capacity to steer their education systems (see Chapter 4). Multilateral agencies, NGOs, and businesses' interests and influences can separately or together constitute a powerful policy alternative to state 'failure'. New policy networks and communities are being established through which particular discourses and knowledge flow and gain legitimacy and credibility and 'these processes are located within a global architecture of political relations that not only involves national governments, but also IGOs [World Bank, OECD, International Finance Corporation, World Trade Organisation], transnational corporations and NGOs. Policies are developed, enacted and evaluated in various global networks from where their authority is now partly derived' (Rizvi & Lingard,

2010, p. 338). These are new policy assemblages with a diverse range of participants which exist in a new kind of policy space somewhere between multilateral agencies, national governments, NGOs, think tanks and advocacy groups, consultants, social entrepreneurs and international business, in and beyond the traditional sites and circulations of policy-making. In these new processes of policy, states are changing, being changed and to some extent being residualised, or as Hannam, Sheller and Urry (2006, p. 2) put it, 'the nation itself is being transformed by [such] mobilities'.

Having said that, the interpretive problem in deciding whether these changes constitute a new form of state or are merely adaptations to the existing form remains. Perhaps what we have, as Jessop and others have proposed, is a new hybrid form or mix of bureaucracy, markets and networks that is fashioned 'in the shadow of hierarchy' (Jessop, 1997, 2002; Scharpf, 1994; Whitehead, 2003), and realised in and through the modalities of 'metagovernance'. That is, 'the organisation of the conditions for governance in its broadest sense' (Jessop, 2002, p. 240) (see Chapter 2). As Jessop (2002, p. 203) argues: 'Much will depend on the ways in which new governance mechanisms are linked to the pursuit of changed state goals in new contexts and to the state's capacities to project its power into the wider society'.

So having done some preliminary ground work around the concepts of global policy networks and neo-liberalism, which appear in the book title, let us try to put some building blocks in place which will contribute to a more thoroughgoing analysis of global education policy. In the remainder of this chapter I want to indicate, briefly, some of the existing concepts that are used to explore and explain the global flow of policy ideas – policy transfer, transnational advocacy networks (TANS), policy entrepreneurs and policy assemblages (to which I return in Chapters 2 and 3) and more specifically the role of think tanks – I return to the role of think tanks several times in later chapters. Some of these concepts I want to use directly, others adapt or dispense with or move beyond.

Policy transfer/policy mobility

The term *policy transfer* refers to a diverse ragbag of ideas which attempt to capture and model the ways in which policy knowledge circulates globally. It is an 'umbrella concept' (Stone, 1999) which is used in and which draws upon diverse literatures. It refers to the 'import' of 'innovatory policy developed elsewhere' (Stone, 1999, p. 52) by national policy-making elites; to the imposition of policy by multilateral agencies; and to processes of structural convergence. Policy transfer analysts ask a number of key questions about the mechanisms involved, including 'who are the key actors involved' (Dolowitz & Marsh, 2000, p. 8). However, 'policy businesses' fail to appear in either Dolowitz and Marsh's 'nine main categories' (p. 10) or Stone's (2004) list of eight, although Stone does include consultancy firms. Furthermore, in these contributions and many others, much more attention is paid to identifying the participants and the successes and failures of transfer than to analysing and explaining the processes involved (Dolowitz and Marsh, 2000, p. 7) or to 'local' mediations and interpretations. Thus, here I want to emphasise the mobility of policies rather than their transfer. That is to say, I suggest that policies move through, and are adapted by, networks of social relations or assemblages (see below), involving diverse participants (see below), with a variety of interests, commitments, purposes and influence, which are held together by subscription to a discursive ensemble, which circulates within and is legitimated by these network relations. Transfer is thus in this case an emergent and multiply scaled process (Hannam et al., 2006).

Despite its neglect in the policy transfer literature, business is now directly engaged with education policy in a number of different ways and these engagements are part of a broader set of complex processes affecting education policy, which include new modes of philanthropy and aid for educational development, market processes of capital growth and expansion and the search by business for new opportunities for profit. The relationships involved here cross and erase national boundaries and form the basis for new kinds of *global assemblages* (Ong, 2006) within which new education policies are produced and disseminated. To adapt Ong's meaning somewhat, these *assemblages* are 'sites' of mobilisation 'by diverse groups in motion' (p. 499) and 'new spaces of entangled possibilities' (p. 499) or what Larner (2002) calls 'globalizing micro-spaces' within which new forms of policy and policy expertise are performed.

Education policy networks, policy flows and transnational advocacy

Arguably, the two main axes of global trends in education policy are those of parental choice and the role of 'private' schooling, and the reform of state education systems along managerialist/entrepreneurial lines (see Chapter 2). The first rests on a set of neo-liberal arguments about more or less radical destatisation (Jessop, 2002), subjecting state organisations to competition and/or the handing over of education service delivery to the private sector. The second is more post-neo-liberal in the sense of reasserting the role of the state but in a new form and with new modalities involving a shift from government to governance; that is from bureaucracy to networks; from delivery to contracting. The first involves forms of exogenous and endogenous privatisation (*metaexchange*) and the second, new forms of organisational practice and culture (*metaorganisation*). In the pragmatics of reform the two are typically blended together.

Both axes have strident support from powerful and influential international actors and are disseminated by powerful transnational agencies and groups – the World Bank, IFC, WTO and the OECD in particular. Both are firmly embedded in the generic nostrums of international management consultancies and education businesses (see Ball, 2007; Ball, 2009). Larbi points this out in relation to late developing societies and 'crisis' states:

> ... large international management consultants, accountancy firms and international financial institutions ... have been instrumental in the increasing 'importation' of new management techniques into the public sector. They have played an important role in packaging, selling and implementing NPM techniques, as state agencies contemplating institutional change or strengthening often enlist the services of expert consultants to clarify available options – and recommend courses of action.
>
> (Larbi, 1999, p. 5)

These kinds of activities entail both 'policy entrepreneurship' *and at the same time* processes of policy transfer, and are a mechanism of 'policy convergence'. The consultants and education businesses which participate are delivering 'development' and aid policy (for a potential profit), developing local policy infrastructures, and embedding prevailing western policy discourses, directly or as 'spillovers' into the local policy systems, working with various 'partners'.[4] In general terms the UK, the USA, Australia, Chile, India, New Zealand and in some ways China are probably the most active sites of both axes of reform (but things are moving fast in South-East Asia, in some east and west African countries, and other parts of Europe), and are reform laboratories from which experiments are exported around the world. They are also important sites for the articulation and export of the rhetorics and discourses of reform and the headquarters of many of the major multinational edu-businesses (see Chapters 4 and 5).

Neo-liberal reforms are also 'carried' and spread globally through the activities of transnational advocacy networks. TANS are typically discussed and portrayed within a paradigm of progressive policy solutions, vulnerable constituencies and community empowerment related to human rights and environmental issues in particular. The Centre on Law and Globalisation defines them as 'fluid and open relationships among knowledgeable, committed actors (individuals and organisations). These relationships span nation-state boundaries. They differ from other types of networks in that they exist to promote principled causes, ideas and values. They exist to change international policy as well as make these changes real in the day-to-day lives of ordinary people'.[5]

> Scholars have been slow to recognize either the rationality or the significance of activist networks. Motivated by values rather than by material concerns or professional norms they fall outside of accustomed categories.
>
> (Keck & Sikkink, 1998, p. 1)

TANS are 'communicative structures' organised around the 'shared values' of their members. Furthermore, TANS can be part of a reshaping of political processes at supranational, national and subnational levels, although as a number of analysts have pointed out their activities and impacts vary between nations in relation to institutional arrangements, policy settings and degrees of democratization, especially when considering transitional or late-developing societies (Dalton & Rohrschneider, 2003; Keck & Sikkink, 1998). TANS provide a network of relations for the diffusion of knowledge and information and typically seek to pluralise political authority. They are a 'third force' (Held & McGrew, 2004) and often an extension of domestic social or political movements. Keck and Sikkink (1998, p. 25) see TANS as changing national government behaviour through the exchange of norms, ideas and discourses, and working to change public perception of social problems – in the cases discussed here there is a contribution being made to the construction of consent in relation to the neo-liberal project (Florini, 2000; Harvey, 2005). Keck and Sikkink (1998) identify four types of TAN strategy: information politics (the ability to move politically effective information quickly), symbolic politics (the ability to call up stories and symbols that have relevance to key audiences), leverage politics (the ability to enrol and deploy influential actors) and accountability politics (the ability to bring pressure to bear on political actors to enact their promises). TANS work 'underneath, above and around the state' (Cavett-Goodwin, 2008) but their success, according to Keck and Sikkink, depends on the strength and depth of their networks and the vulnerability of the target state or organisations.

As parts of TANS and sometimes in their own right, think tanks often have very specific and effective points of entry into political systems: 'think tanks are nested in a web of relationships'. The possibilities for impact and influence are magnified through network interactions (Stone, 2008, p. 9). Wapner (1996) also notes that: 'The authority and legitimacy for think tank involvement in global affairs is not naturally given but has been cultivated and groomed through various management practices and intellectual activities'. She goes on to say that 'In some cases, however, the think tank scholarly "aura" and independence may be misleading ... in reality ideas become harnessed to political and economic interests'. Stone also makes the point that 'Whilst the global expansion and networking of think tanks has contributed to an increasingly diverse and plural community it has also created new hierarchies. The internationally prominent institutes tend to be Western organizations, or at least, those institutes based in OECD countries' (Stone, 2008, p. 8).

On the whole, the TANS literature tends to neglect the role of individual policy entrepreneurs (PEs) (see Oborn, Barrett & Exworthy (2011) for a full discussion of the use of the concept). However, Stone (2000, p. 216) suggests that PEs perform three functions. They identify needs and offer innovative means to satisfy them; they bear financial and emotional risks in pursing change where consequences are uncertain; and they assemble and coordinate networks of individuals and organisations with the talents and resources needed to achieve change. The personal resources needed by the policy entrepreneur 'include intellectual ability, knowledge of policy matters, leadership and team-building skills, reputation and contacts, strategic ability, and tenacity' (Mintrom & Vergari, 1996, p. 424), particular forms and volumes of social and cultural capital which can be reinvested in policy activity. Thus, policy entrepreneurship focuses on the role of agency in policy-making and policy mobility (Oborn, Barrett and Exworthy, 2011, p. 326), the work of 'activists with a particular interest in the success of the policy' (John, 2003, p. 493). The policy entrepreneur is adept at constructing or opening and taking advantage of 'policy windows' (Kingdon, 1995). Policy entrepreneurs, as Kingdon puts it, 'lie in wait' (p. 181) and so need to be ready, flexible and persistent, and be able to 'hook solutions to problems, proposals to political momentum and political events to policy problems' (p. 182). All of the contributions to the literature make the point that such people are few and far between – certainly only a handful are identified in this analysis. The problem here, especially in the relationships between policy entrepreneurship and policy windows, is that there is both a little too much emphasis on agency and not enough. Too much emphasis, in the sense that the focus on entrepreneurship tends to underemphasise the role of discourses and the role of economics. Policy windows are, in part at least, constructed discursively, and specifically here windows are created within the processes and activities and ideological critiques of 'proto' and 'roll-back' neo-liberalism. Furthermore, these critiques, as we will see in the following chapter, are typically 'fully funded' and strategically articulated. Too little emphasis, in the sense, and in the same vein, that effective policy entrepreneurship is destructive as well as creative – there is nothing so productive for change as a good crisis and its attendant 'moral panics'. Policy problems are as often as not 'constructed' rather than identified.

> Problematization doesn't mean the representation of a pre-existent object, nor the creation through discourse of an object that doesn't exist. It's the set of discursive or nondiscursive practices that makes something enter into the play of the true and false, and constitutes it as an object for thought (whether under the form of moral reflection, scientific knowledge, political analysis, etc.).
>
> (Michel Foucault, interview with Francis Ewald, 'The concern for truth', *Le Magazine Littéraire*, May 1984, pp. 456–57)

Generally, with some exceptions, in the literature indicated in this section the dangers of what Jessop, Brenner & Jones (2008) call 'flat ontology' are very much in evidence. Influence and intervention are portrayed as virtually frictionless and lacking in 'spatially sensitive explanations of more concrete-complex phenomena' (p. 392). In other words, there is a failure to ground the work of advocacy in specific practices, in specific locations, involving lived social relations and interactions and costs. There is a conflation of space and place. In saying that I am very aware of Peck and Tickell's (2002) point that in the analysis of neo-liberalism and its effectivities we always have to 'walk the line between local specificity and global interconnection'.

Neo-liberalism is not simply, as some writers portray it, a process of privatization, individualization and state attrition, although those are important components. Neo-liberalism also works on and in public sector institutions, and on and in the state – indeed the state is important to neo-liberalism as regulator and market-maker. The paradoxes of this are discussed and examined in the following chapter. Neo-liberalism is also realised, disseminated and embedded through quasi-markets, Public Private Partnerships, the 'enterprising-up' of public organisations, and the work of charities and voluntary organisations, indeed the third sector can be seen as a new governmentality being rolled out under neo-liberalism (Graefe, 2005; Rose, 1999).

These sorts of practices and the new forms of governance that they entail were a central aspect of New Labour public sector reforms in England (the Third Way, 1997–2010) and are also a major basis of current Conservative/ Coalition policies for public sector 'change' (the Big Society). However, they are also being played out globally through the growth of 'social enterprise' solutions to 'wicked' educational and social problems and the activities of global social actors like the Clinton Global Initiative (see Chapter 4) and through the interests and ambition of national and global edu-businesses (see Chapter 6). Education is just one manifestation of a global reworking of the economic, social, moral and political foundations of public service provision and the development of new kinds of political responses to social disadvantage. In the rest of the book some of this varied and complex terrain will be mapped and explored in relation to education policy.

Chapter 2 focuses on the ambiguous tensions between the market and the state which are central to the neo-liberal project – less state and more markets. This is done in two ways. First, by looking at the neo-liberal advocacy work of the Atlas Liberty Network. Second, by looking at the neo-liberalising of the state itself, through the technologies of performativity, leadership and enterprise. The point is that neo-liberal reform is both exogenous (privatising) and endogenous (reforming), the public sector is replaced and reformed, at the same time, and the two things are connected. Chapter 3 examines a very specific and located network of neo-liberal advocacy focused on educational reform in India and on the work of a set of organisations animated by policy entrepreneur James Tooley. The intention here is to demonstrate the work of neo-liberalism, the connectivity of its agents and organisations, and the mobility of policy. Chapter 4 takes this focus further, concentrating in particular on the methods and relationships of 'new' philanthropy and global social capitalism. That is, the application, via venture philanthropy, of market solutions to 'wicked' social problems. Some network connections around the founding and funding of private schools for the poor in Africa are traced. Chapter 5 is about policy as a commodity and identifies three levels of involvement of global edu-business in policy work – the retail selling of policy translations; the outsourcing of 'statework'; and the buying and selling of policy ideas. Chapter 6 looks at buying and selling in another sense, through the business strategies of multinational edu-businesses, management service organisations and private-equity companies. The chapter also seeks to indicate the ways in which 'roll-back' and 'roll-out' neo-liberalism are joined up between advocacy, non-for-profit and business organisations – distinctions are blurred and effects achieved. Chapter 7 revisits some of the key concepts employed in the analysis and presents an overview of the neo-liberalisation of global education policy.

Of necessity and by design the boundaries between the chapters are porous. The book is about mobility and connectivity. That is, how policy ideas are joined up and how they move. I am seeking to portray a set of complex relationships between organisations, actors, ideas, locations and activities that cannot be neatly divided up or divided off from one another. That is the point – we need to 'see' education policy and governance on a different scale and through new conceptual lenses; neatness is not an option.

Notes

1 Project nos. RES-000-27-0090 and RES-000-22-2682.
2 Ball 2010a.
3 A significant subset of this literature draws upon and relates specifically to the development of multi-level forms of governance within Europe. Given that European policy is developed within networks characterised by a hybrid mix of individual actors embedded in a system of national, subnational, supra-national, intergovernmental and transnational relations, the European literature sees 'policy networks as a real change in the structure of the polity' (Besussi, 2006, p. 6).
4 The complexity of these roles, relationships, models of working and under-pinning principles makes it difficult to distinguish between public and private in a simple way.
5 clg.portalxm.com/library/keytext.cfm?keytext_id=113   (accessed   24   March 2009).

2   Doing neo-liberalism – markets and states, and friends with money

Opposing the state has become an industry.
(Richard Cornuelle, Volker Fund, interview quoted in Doherty, 2007, p. 591)

One way of thinking about and researching neo-liberalism is as 'a trans-national pressure to release economic activity from state regulation' (Olssen, Codd & O'Neill, 2004) or as something that 'puts into question all collective structures capable of obstructing the logic of the pure market' (Tabb, 2002). Thus, one of the recurrent points of reference in this account of global education policy and neo-liberal practices is the fundamental antagonism and, at the same time, mutual dependency between markets and states. It is not possible to account for the roll-out of 'actually existing' neo-liberalism without also addressing changes to the form and modalities of the state. These changes are taking place at the nexus between regulation and midwifery (Blackmore, 1999), that is the role of the state in setting limits to the market, while at the same time creating conditions within which the market can flourish and expand – there are many examples of this duality in the chapters which follow. In its current iteration this duality of regulation and facilitation is expressed and enacted by means of what Jessop calls *metagovernance* – 'the organisation of the conditions for governance in its broadest sense' (2002, p. 240). Metagovernance represents a shift in state organisation and practices, which in political science is commonly referred to as a shift from government to governance. That is:

> The hierarchical model of government is in decline, pushed by governments' appetites to solve ever more complicated problems and pulled by new tools that allow innovators to fashion creative responses. This push and pull is gradually producing a new government model, in which executives' core responsibilities no longer centre on managing people and programs but on organising resources—often belonging to others—to produce public value.
> (William D. Eggers, 'The Changing Nature of Government: Network Governance', http://epress.anu.edu.au/anzsog/collab_gov/mobile_devices/ch03.html, accessed 21 February 2011)

Extending this rather arcane and tangled vocabulary further, Jessop goes on to outline three basic modes of metagovernance. These are *metaexchange, metaorganisation* and *metaheterarchy*. I want to suggest here that these modes, working together, produce the general and generic technologies and techniques of the neo-liberal state, and that these technologies and techniques also constitute the specific operating principles of contemporary global education policy, what Spring (2008) calls 'global uniformity'. In the second part of this chapter I will briefly outline each mode, point out some of their interconnections and indicate the ways in which they provide the conditions for the *neo-liberalisation* of education and for governing education.

Before getting to that I want first to spend a little time on the other side of the duality – in the market, or at least in looking a little more closely at the market doctrine, and at how the state is viewed and represented or 'misrepresented' (Brenner & Theodore, 2002, p. 353) by market advocates. I want to do this in a particular way, that is, by focusing on the tenets, rhetorics and methods of a particular set of neo-liberal or libertarian advocates, specifically the Atlas Foundation and its Liberty Network – a very particular and purposeful TAN. In this way we can explore the market and neo-liberalism from the viewpoint of advocacy and its practices – as discussed in the previous chapter – and not just as a set of free-floating ideas. The spread and take-up of neo-liberal practices rests upon a great deal of political and ideological work that is highly organised and well funded. Brenner and Theodore assert that:

> First, neoliberal doctrine represents states and markets as if they were diametrically opposed principles of social organisation, rather than recognizing the politically constructed character of all economic relations. Second, neoliberal doctrine is premised on a 'one size fits all' model of policy implementation ...
>
> (Brenner & Theodore, 2002, p. 353)

It is generally the case that neo-liberalism is used to refer to a family of ideas associated with the revival of nineteenth-century economic liberalism. This normally includes the school of Austrian economics associated with von Mises, Hayek and Schumpeter, the Chicago School of economists, and monetarist economist Milton Friedman, but in some versions also draws upon the libertarian ideas of writers like Ayn Rand and Murray Rothbard, and more recently Frédéric Bastiat. It is characterised by a strong commitment to methodological individualism and the principles of private property, alongside an antipathy to centralised state planning – or *minarchism* as it is sometimes called, the idea that government should be limited to defence, adjudication and a very limited provision of public goods, and based on an anti-rationalist epistemology. Let us look at these doctrines as articulated in the 'mission' of and 'at work' within the Liberty Network and its members and partners, and take one brief local example of dissemination and advocacy through the Network as can be traced through to its members' organisations in Brazil.

The Atlas Economic Research Foundation

It is only possible to glimpse and sample here the complex, interlinked network relations of which Atlas is a part. What I can do is to indicate some of the (many) threads and relationships which work through the Atlas Liberty Network, some of which are taken up and taken further in the following chapters. In effect we will look at one cross-section of Atlas relations and activities, a small slice across a massive range of diverse and multifaceted events, mobilities, interactions and connections, by following some of the 'arrows' which connect up elements within the network. In doing this some key actors and organisations can be introduced and their 'concerns' with educational issues can be signalled. To an extent this is a ready-made network but beyond the official on-site listings of partner organisations there are many more indirect, interpersonal and occasional relationships, partnerships, joint activities and meeting points between like-minded free-market, libertarian organisations and people. Nonetheless, libertarianism is a broad and diverse church and in his book *Radicals For Capitalism*, Doherty (2007) gives a fulsome, insider's account of the inter-necine and contentious struggles which take place within the libertarian movement. However, he also makes the point that today 'more money is flowing into the libertarian movement, more people are making their living from professional libertarian activism, and more academic research is being done in libertarian directions all the time' (p. 579).

Atlas has its headquarters in Arlington Virginia and, according to its website (all quotations below from http://atlasnetwork.org as of 25 October 2011), has launched or nurtured and connects 'a global network of more than 400 free-market organizations in over 80 countries to the ideas and resources needed to advance the cause of liberty'. On the Atlas website these organisations can be viewed by country and examined individually through weblinks. The mission of Atlas, according to John Blundell (one time Director General of the Institute of Economic Affairs in London, Director of the London-based International Policy Network, and board member of the Mont Pelerin Society, and Atlas' president from 1987 to 1990), 'is to litter the world with free-market think-tanks'. Atlas presents a simple message easily understood by politicians and policy-makers in diverse locations. Atlas believes that 'the prospects for free societies all over the world depend upon "intellectual entrepreneurs" in civil society, who wish to improve public policy debates through sound research'. It aims 'To discover, develop and support "intellectual entrepreneurs" worldwide who can advance the Atlas vision of a society of free and responsible individuals'. To this end Atlas also runs or supports four Free Enterprise Training Centers that 'conduct "training programs" for young people to sharpen their understanding of the

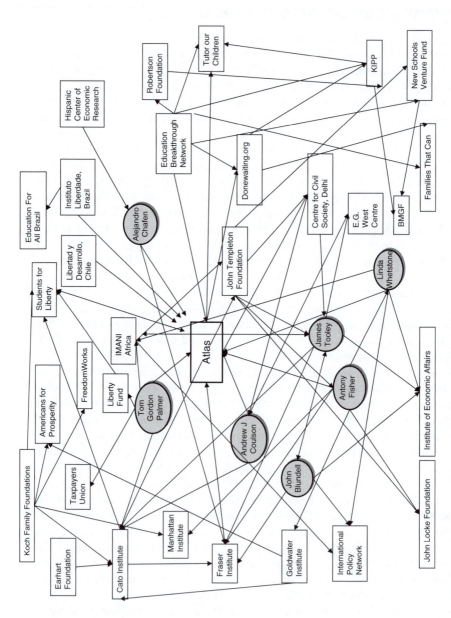

Figure 2.1 The Atlas Economic Research Foundation.

ideas of liberty and the role think tanks play to advance liberty over the long-term' – they are based in Libertad y Desarrollo (Chile), Lithuanian Free Market Institute, Association for Liberal Thinking (Turkey) and Nadacia F. A. Hayeka Bratislava (Slovakia). Hayek is a key and recurrent source of inspiration and ideas for Atlas and its members. Atlas also runs an annual Liberty Forum, which brings together liberal thinkers from think tanks around the world and Atlas events feature prominent intellectual leaders of libertarian thought, such as Milton Friedman, Hernando de Soto, José María Aznar, Mart Laar, Charles Murray, Walter Williams and Francisco Flores. The Forum is now timed to coincide with the Liberty Dinner. As reported by the Asia Economic Freedom Network (http://www.efnasia.org, accessed 25 July 2011), The Liberty Dinner 2010 celebrated

> the fall of the Berlin Wall and honours the courageous individuals who stood for liberty in the face of communism. The Liberty Forum features education specialist Lisa Keegan of Education Breakthrough Network, economist Gabriel Calzada of Instituto Juan de Mariana in Spain, fundraising guru Ann Fitzgerald of A.C. Fitzgerald & Associates, public relations and advertising sage Rick Berman of Berman and Company, bio-chemist and author Terence Kealey of the University of Buckingham (UK) and Toasts to Freedom from Atlas's think tank partners from around the world.

The Education Breakthrough Network is a school choice advocacy organisation which partners with National School Choice Week, Donewaiting.org and Tutor our Children, to provide information and support to school choice developments in the USA. Breakthrough is linked to many other pro-choice and Charter school organisations like KIPP, Families That Can and the New Schools Venture Fund.

> The Network is a very detailed site, explaining who provides school choices, who advocates for students, teachers, and families to have greater choice, and offering extensive video and Google maps to seek out a school, organization, or advocate near you.
> (http://www.edbreakthrough.org/aboutus.php, accessed 25 July 2011)

Through events and connections like these Atlas is the focus of a formidable network of power, influence, ideas and money, it interrelates to other networks, websites, blogs and publications which share its commitment to liberty, entrepreneurship and 'limited government' – Students for Limited Government is an Atlas partner and a subset of Students for Liberty [SFL].

> SFL has partnered with Atlas to introduce the 19th century French political scientist, Frédéric Bastiat, and launch the Bastiat Project-a

multi-faceted effort that includes the production of the book, *The Economics of Freedom: What Your Professors Won't Tell You*, for mass distribution, an essay contest, and more.

(http://atlasnetwork.org/blog/2010/08/washington-d-c-braving-the-storm-students-for-limited-government, accessed 25 July 2011)

Atlas has awarded grants of over $20m; through its website it offers think tank leadership training, a think tank toolkit and a think tank primer, with contributions from think tank leaders around the world. It also runs an Outreach and Discovery Program:

> The Atlas Outreach and Discovery Program creates, manages, and promotes products and programs in a number of languages and encourages worldwide cooperation among those who understand and value liberty. It helps facilitate a worldwide network across disparate countries that advances aspirations for individual liberty, freedom of association, religious freedom, freedom of trade, limited government, the rule of law, and peace.

Atlas was launched in 1981 by Antony Fisher, a British chicken farmer who was also co-founder in the UK of the Hayekian Institute of Economic Affairs (see Chapter 3). Fisher was also involved in the launch of ICEPS, which later became the Manhattan Institute in the US, and helped to found the Pacific Research Institute and the Fraser Institute (Canada). Atlas also aided the creation of the Goldwater Institute, the Acton Institute, the John Locke Foundation and several other think tanks which are united in their commitment to libertarian economic thought, that can, as Doherty (2007) puts it, 'be seen as representing either the libertarianizing of conservative activism or the conservatization of libertarian activism' (p. 479). Atlas is funded from a variety of sources including the John Templeton Foundation and the Templeton Freedom Awards have been given by Atlas since 2004. The awards honour free-market think tanks. In addition:

> The Atlas Network has partnered with the John Templeton Foundation on a new and important project – The Morality of Free Enterprise – that will build on the Templeton Foundation's online conversation, 'Does the Free Market Corrode Moral Character?'

Alejandro Chafuen was elected President of Atlas in 2009. Chafuen served as Atlas's CEO from 1991 to 2009. He founded the Hispanic American Center of Economic Research and wrote the book *Faith and Liberty*. He has served on the boards of the Chase Foundation, the Acton Institute and the Fraser Institute. He has been a faculty member at the Argentine Catholic University, the University of Buenos Aires, and the Hispanic American University in California.

Organisations which Atlas has supported (a full list can be found on the Liberty Network website) include:

Fraser Institute (Canada)
Buckeye Institute
National Center for Policy Analysis
Center for the Dissemination of Economic Information in Venezuela
Centre for Independent Studies
Centro Interdisciplinar de Ética e Economia Personalista, in Brazil
Adam Smith Institute (UK)
Lion Rock Institute, Hong Kong
Hispanic American Center for Economic Research (HACER)
Andes Libres, Peru, African Research Institute for Public Policy and
    Market Process in Kenya
Free Market Center, Belgrade, Serbia
Civic Institute in Prague
Centre for Civil Society (India)*
Circle of Tradition and Progress, London
Liberty Institute, New Delhi*
Liberty Institute, Romania
Unirule, Beijing
Instituto Liberdade Brazil http://www.il-rs.org.br/ilingles/index.htm
Instituto de Estudos Empresariais Brazil
Environment Probe, Canada http://www.environmentprobe.org
New Economic School – Georgia
Institute for Democracy and Economic Affairs, Malaysia
                    *National Institute for Information and Technology

Think tanks such as these within the Network are nodes for the circulation and reiteration of publications and ideas and the advocacy of free-market and libertarian social and economic policies. Themes, issues and reports and papers and policy proposals – like school choice – recur and repeat in each location. Atlas also has strong links with the Cato Institute:

> The Cato Institute is a public policy research organisation – a think tank – dedicated to the principles of individual liberty, limited government, free markets and peace. Its scholars and analysts conduct independent, non-partisan research on a wide range of policy issues.
>
> (www.cato.org/)

Tom Gordon Palmer, Atlas's Vice President for International Programs, is a Senior Fellow at the Cato Institute, and was director of the Institute's educational division, the Cato University. He is also General Director of the Atlas Global Initiative for Free Trade, Peace, and Prosperity. He has been editor of several publications, including *Dollars & Sense* (the newspaper

of the National Taxpayers Union), *Update* and the *Humane Studies Review*.
He teaches political economy and legal and constitutional history for the
Institute for Humane Studies and the Institute of Economic Studies Europe.
He also works with such organisations as Liberty Fund and the Council on
Public Policy. Cato itself has been supported financially by dozens of phi-
lanthropic foundations including:

Atlantic Philanthropies
Charles G. Koch Charitable Foundation
Earhart Foundation
JM Foundation, founded by Jeremiah Milbank
John M. Olin Foundation, Inc.
Claude R. Lambe Charitable Foundation
Lynde and Harry Bradley Foundation
Castle Rock Foundation (formerly known as The Coors Foundation)
Scaife Foundations (Sarah Mellon Scaife, Carthage)
Ford Foundation
Ploughshares Fund

Each of these funders would bear careful attention but we have space to
note just two. The Earhart Foundation was founded in 1929 by the president of the White Star Oil Company, and supports with grants the work
of 'promising' intellectuals to become academic leaders and teachers –
Fredrick Von Hayek was a beneficiary. The Claude R Lambe Charitable
Foundation is now part of and is run by the Koch Family Foundations,
which were established with the stated purpose of advancing social progress
and well-being through the development, application and dissemination
of 'the Science of Liberty'. The Koch foundations have together provided
millions of dollars to a variety of organisations, usually libertarian or conservative think tanks, such as the Americans for Prosperity Foundation, the
Mercatus Center, the Institute for Humane Studies, Citizens for a Sound
Economy, the Institute for Justice, the Alexis de Tocqueville Institution, the
Institute for Energy Research, the Foundation for Research on Economics
and the Environment, the Heritage Foundation, the Manhattan Institute,
the George C. Marshall Institute, the Reason Foundation and the American
Enterprise Institute. Doherty (2007, p. 410) describes Koch's funding as
'a means to increase the amount of libertarian capital goods in order to
create more of the ultimate political consumer good of libertarian policy'.
Recent Cato 'Studies' include:

'Edupreneurs:' A Survey of For-Profit Education
The Other Lottery: Are Philanthropists Backing the Best Charter Schools?
They Spend WHAT? The Real Cost of Public Schools
The Poverty of Preschool Promises: Saving Children and Money with the
    Early Education Tax Credit

Reclaiming Our Schools: Increasing Parental Control of Education
through the Universal Education Credit

The current website (25 July 2011) also contains an article from the Swedish newspaper *Svenska Dagbladet* on Swedish Free Schools, written by Cato's
Andrew J. Coulson, which includes this:

> ... a recent study by London's Institute for Economic Affairs reveals
> that Swedish private schools are significantly outperforming govern-
> ment schools academically. According to official enrollment figures,
> private schools are also gaining market share from government schools –
> so the better schools are growing and crowding out the less effective
> ones. Excellence is 'scaling-up'.

Andrew J. Coulson directs the Cato Institute's Center for Educational
Freedom in Washington, DC, and is author of *Market Education: The
Unknown History*. Previously, he was senior fellow in Education Policy at
the Mackinac Center for Public Policy. He serves on the Advisory Council
of the E.G. West Centre for Market Solutions in Education at the University
of Newcastle, UK (see Chapter 3) and has contributed to books published
by the Fraser Institute and the Hoover Institution. He is friend and collaborator of private school school choice advocate James Tooley (see Chapters 2
and 3). Like Tooley, Coulson is an advocate of the development of private
schools for the poor in India but a critic of India's Right to Education Act,
which seeks to both recognize and regulate these schools; he describes this
attempt at regulation as a 'looming catastrophe'. Coulson's blog includes
this comment, first published on *The Huffington Post,* which returns to the
main theme of this chapter – the antagonisms of markets and states:

> This looming catastrophe has been recognized by the New Delhi-based
> Center for Civil Society, which, among other groups, has filed suit
> to block the RtE [Right to Education] Act regulations that would
> eradicate low-cost entrepreneurial education in India. But such matters
> needn't be decided in a courtroom. The evidence that government reg-
> ulation fails to improve educational quality is extensive and readily
> available. Just as clear is the successful and growing role played by
> unrecognized entrepreneurial private schools that are held accountable
> directly by parents. The law can be changed to reflect these realities
> if the people demand it.
> (http://leagueofindia.com/blog/premjis-gift-and-future-education-india,
> accessed 25 October 2010)

Coulson's tweets (http://twitter.com/#!/Andrew_Coulson) focus in particular
on issues of school choice, vouchers, private schooling and the 'failures'
of the public school system. He refers often on Twitter and in his

publications to James Tooley's work as exemplifying the possibility of private schooling – Cato published Tooley's book *The Beautiful Tree* in the US (see Chapter 3).

The point here is to illustrate something of the discursive and epistemic density and connectivity of the networks which are linked to and through Atlas and the range of activities and interventions in which Atlas and its collaborators are engaged (and which will also be apparent in Chapter 3) and their global reach. We also see something of the funding streams which underwrite these activities, most of which flow from family foundations whose income derives from US national and multinational capital. I hope also to have conveyed some sense of the family of concepts and commitments which are invested in and continually reaffirmed through these flows and connections – liberty, individualism, responsibility, enterprise and entrepreneurism, market solutions and market freedom, limited government, consumer choice and tax reductions. This is a purposeful agenda which is translated into policy proposals, lobbying and influence in government, the media and academia. These root commitments also join up in places to other moral and political positions, like the Templeton Foundation's quasi-fundamentalist interests in the morality of capitalism and 'intelligent design', Cato's opposition to the Iraq war and 'imperial' foreign policy, Koch's stance on gun law, scepticism about global warming (see Reason. com – Free minds and Free markets), the Manhattan Institute and Charles Murray's opposition to welfare (*Losing Ground*), and Murray's racist IQism (*The Bell Curve*) – from which both Manhattan and Cato sought to distance themselves. Through its advocacy and policy work Atlas plays a significant role in the roll-back and roll-out activities of neo-liberalism, that is in both destabilising welfare policies and welfare thinking and creating new spaces for market activity and fostering consent around ideas of choice and market freedom, and latterly, and to a lesser extent, to stabilising or further entrenching neo-liberalism through the introduction of new institutions, policies and governmentalities. The Liberty Network is a mode of advocacy and set of relationships for moving ideas around and for joining up ideas to spaces of change, increasingly so in late developing societies and the BRICs. The point is to make 'the market' the obvious solution to social and economic problems. The tactic is to work locally and globally, to enable voices for change which can be made a part of local political systems, by bringing ideas, relationships and money to bear. This advocacy is also linked to the very real and particular interests of business (as we shall see in Chapter 3) and some actors move between the world of political ideas and the world of profit.

Atlas, Liberty and Brazil

There are about 7 Brazilian members of the Liberty Network (the membership changes); they include the Instituto Millenium, Instituto Liberal,

Instituto Liberdade, Instituto Altantico, the Mises Institute and Instituto de Estudos Empresariais. Here Austrian economics and Milton Friedman are key points of reference. One of these, the Instituto Liberdade, was 2006 Winner of the Templeton Freedom Award for Institutional Excellence. The Instituto Liberdade's major purpose is:

> To foster the research, creation and dissemination of educational and cultural assets displaying the advantages to all individuals of an organized society, based on the principles of individual rights, of limited and representative government, of respect to private property rights, contracts and to the free initiative. It supports multi-disciplinary theorists and intellectual entrepreneurs who endeavor to produce analyses or policy recommendations. It supports the rule of the law, the government decentralization, the free market economy, the cultural freedom according to the principles of the Austrian School of Economics.
>
> (Instituto Liberdade website)

Liberdade has published articles and collaborated with other think tanks in reports and studies, such as the Civil Society Report on Intellectual Property; Free Trade in the Americas from the International Policy Network; Friedrich Naumann Foundation; Competitive Enterprise Institute; Montreal Economic Institute; Instituto de Estudos Empresariais; Institute of Economic Affairs; and the Inter-American Policy Exchange at the Manhattan Institute. Some of the values, aims and flow of ideas of the Instituto Liberdade (and the other Institutos) are fairly self-evident in the 'information' offered to visitors interested in *Project School Choice*; approximately 100 papers and reports are listed, including:

Why America Needs School Choice   18/07/2011
School Choice and State Constitutions: A Guide to Designing School
    Choice Programs   21/06/2011
Are Unions a Benefit or Obstacle to the Education of Children?
    02/06/2011
10 Questions State Legislators Should Ask About Higher Education
    26/05/2011
How Much Do Public Schools Spend on Teaching?   19/05/2011
Beyond Good and Evil: Understanding the Role of For-Profits in
    Education through the Theories of Disruptive Innovation
    19/05/2011
Who Subsidizes Whom? An Analysis of Educational Costs and Revenues
    18/04/2011
From School Choice to Educational Choice   14/04/2011
School Choice Works   29/03/2011
Why Massachusetts Should Double the Number of Charter Schools
    28/03/2011

A Win-Win Solution: The Empirical Evidence on School Vouchers
     23/03/2011
Who Should Decide How Children are Educated?   18/03/2011
Ten Principles of Higher Education Reform   14/03/2011
School Choice Is Back   09/03/2011
The ABCs of School Choice   24/02/2011
A Chronology of School Choice in the U.S.   23/02/2011
15 School Choice Myths

The current events calendar (25 July 2011) includes the following, which indicate some of the organisational structures and intellectual flows which animate the Liberty Network.

Mont Pelerin Society General Conference 2012   02/09/2012
35th Annual Resource Bank Meeting from The Heritage Foundation
     26/04/2012
The Atlas Experience 2012   25/04/2012
Freedom Dinner and Templeton Freedom Awards Ceremony
     09/11/2011
Atlas Liberty Forum 2011 and 30th anniversary celebration
     08/11/2011
Think Tank Leadership Training   06/11/2011
Spring Master Program – TU Dortmund University   10/10/2011
2011 Economic Freedom of the World Annual Conference   05/10/2011
Austrian Economics Autumn School   30/09/2011
Celebration 20th Anniversary of IEEP   04/08/2011
2011 Challenge of Liberty Summer Seminars/College Student Seminar
     01/08/2011
2011 Bastiat Prize – Win $50,000   31/07/2011
The Friedman Legacy for Freedom   29/07/2011
Sharing the Legacy and Ideas of Milton Friedman   29/07/2011
CATO University Summer Seminar on Political Economy

These Institutes are local conduits in an international network of relations for the diffusion of knowledge and information – 'one fits all' neo-liberalism – and are changing national government thinking and behaviour through the exchange of norms, ideas and discourses, and are working to change public perception of social problems in Brazil, including education. As a specific example of such work, one of Instituto Liberdade's many partner organisations is *Todos pela Educação (Education for All)*. The Education for All programme was founded by the presidents of several Brazilian companies, including the DPaschoal car parts chain, the Gerdau Group and major banks Itaú, Bradesco and Santander. The project/programme, now adopted by the Brazilian government, has developed goals for Brazil's education and introduced performance monitoring tools with the help of US and Brazilian education experts. Education for All has also used academic and media channels to help promote education as a national priority. The president of *Todos pela Educação* Jorge Gerdau Johannpeter, Chairman and President of Gerdau S.A., is also a member of the council of the Instituto Millenium.

This example provides a neat link back to the main theme of this chapter – the complex and changing relationships between the market, the state and the public sector. As indicated earlier, these relationships are invested with both antagonism and interdependence. As Harvey (2005, p. 2) explains:

> ... if markets do not exist (in areas such as land, water, education, health care, social security and environmental pollution) then they must be created, by state action if necessary. But beyond these tasks the state should not venture. State interventions in markets (once created) must be kept to a bare minimum because according to the theory, the state cannot possibly possess enough information to second-guess market signals (prices) and because powerful interest groups will inevitably distort and bias state interventions (particularly in democracies) for their own benefit.

What I want to go on to do is to explore aspects of these relationships and tensions through what we might call *the neo-liberalising of the state.*

Neo-liberalism and metagovernance

I want to sketch some of the practices and technologies through which neo-liberalism operates in and on educational institutions – some of which will be returned to in more detail in later chapters. Attending to these practices will also begin to help us think about the ways in which neo-liberalism is realised in mundane and immediate ways in our institutions of everyday life, and the ways it 'does us' – speaks and acts through our language, purposes, decisions and social relations. That is, as Peck (2003) argues, neo-liberalism is 'in here' as well as 'out there'. In thinking about these practices we can also think about how we are 'reformed' by neo-liberalism, made into different kinds of educational workers, and how endogenous changes in public sector organisations make possible, that is lay the groundwork for, exogenous substitution – the privatization, in different forms, of public education services. At its most visceral and intimate, neo-liberalism involves the transformation of social relations into calculabilities and exchanges, that is into the market form, and thus the commodification of educational practice – e.g. in economies of student worth, through performance-related pay, performance management and flexibilisation and labour replacement (see Ball, 2008a). Neo-liberal technologies work on us to produce 'docile and productive' teacher and the student bodies, and responsible and enterprising teacher and the student selves.

Attention to the mundane also serves to highlight neo-liberalism as a process, not something that is realised as a set of grand strategies and ruptural changes but rather made up of numerous moves, incremental reforms, displacements and reinscriptions, complicated and stuttering trajectories of small changes and tactics which work together on systems, organisations and individuals – to make these isomorphic. They are made into enterprises. These ensembles of changes work together to produce new practices, subjectivities and 'opportunities'. This constitutes a process of attrition which gradually renders the social into the commodity form and amenable to profit. Neo-liberalism is also polymorphic and evolving, it morphs and adapts, taking on local characteristics from the geographies of existing political economic circumstances and institutional frameworks, where variability, internal constitution, societal influences and individual agency all play a role in (re)producing, circulating, and facilitating its advance. It can 'materialise' differently in mutated and hybrid forms. Thus, the technologies discussed below are evident to different degrees, in different forms, in different places, at different points in time. In education, we might say that there is a neo-liberal curriculum of reform.

The neo-liberal curriculum of reform

'curriculum is the course of experience(s) that forms human beings into persons'.

The 'curriculum' here is about the public sector learning to confront its purported inadequacies, learning lessons from the methods and values of the private sector, and learning to reform itself. As well as in another sense learning the 'hard lessons' taught by the disciplines of the market. All of this involves the instilling of new sensibilities and values, and new forms of social relations, into the practices of the public sector. The private sector is the model to be emulated, and the public sector is to be 'enterprised' in its image.

In practice the neo-liberal curriculum consists of a set of moral technologies which work on, in and through public sector institutions and workers. These technologies are complexly interrelated and I have written about them before (e.g. Ball, 2001a, 2003b, etc.). Here, as indicated above, we can think about them as aspects of metagovernance, forms and means of governing by organising the conditions for governing – metaorganisation, metaexchange and metaheterarchy. These are closely interrelated, and in particular measurement, or to be more precise *performativity*, is a key aspect and integrating technique of these interrelationships, and is a vital component of both management and enterprise. At the level of institutional practice, performativity facilitates and requires the reflexive redesign of organisations, organisational relationships and organisational ecologies. In effect organisations are 'enabled' to think about themselves differently, in terms of, or in relation to their performance.

Performativity is a term that is increasingly widely used in policy analysis and writing, but it is not always used in its full and proper sense. What I mean by that is that the usefulness of the concept is not just as another way of referring to systems of performance management but it addresses also the work that performance management systems do on the subjectivities of practitioners. Indeed, performativity is the quintessential form of neo-liberal governmentality, which encompasses subjectivity, institutional practices, economy and government. It is both individualizing and totalizing. It produces both an active docility and depthless productivity. Performativity invites and incites us to make ourselves more effective, to work on ourselves, to improve ourselves and to feel guilty or inadequate if we do not. It operates within a framework of judgement within which what 'improvement' and effectiveness are, is determined for us, and 'indicated' of us by measures of quality and productivity. Performativity is enacted through measures and targets against which we are expected to position ourselves but often in ways that also produce uncertainties about how we should organise ourselves within our work. Shore and Wright (1999) even go as far as to suggest that these uncertainties are a tactic for the destabilization of the public sector. Performativity 'works' most powerfully when it is inside our heads and our souls. That is, when we do it to ourselves, when we take responsibility for working hard, faster and better, thus 'improving' our 'output', as part of our sense of personal worth and the worth of others. Also then it is important to recognise that performative systems offer us the possibility of being better than we were or even being the excellent – and better than others – in its own terms. Performativity is not in any simple sense a technology of oppressions; it is also one of satisfactions and rewards, at least for some. Performativity is a key mechanism of neo-liberal management, a form of hands-off management that uses comparisons and judgements in place of interventions and direction. As Davies (2005) puts it: 'The language and practices of neoliberal managerialism are seductive. They lay the grounds for new kinds of success and recognition' (p. 8). Indeed, performativity works best when we come to want for ourselves what is wanted from us, when our moral sense of our desires and ourselves are aligned with its pleasures. In a sense it is about making the individual into an enterprise, as suggested above, a self-maximising productive unit operating in a market of performances – committed to the 'headlong pursuit of relevance as defined by the market' (Falk, 1999, p. 25). The neo-liberal subject is malleable rather than committed, flexible rather than principled – essentially depthless. A consequence of continual animation and calculation is for many a growing sense of ontological insecurity; both a loss of a sense of meaning in what we do and of what is important in what we do.

Within all this the organisation – school, college, university, agency – and the person are treated in exactly the same way. The self-managing individual and the autonomous organisation are produced within the interstices of performativity through audits, inspections, appraisals, self-reviews, quality assurance, research assessments, output indicators and so on. We and our workplace are made visible and we become 'subjects which have to be seen' (Foucault, 1979, p. 187). These individual techniques and devices taken as a whole constitute a political economy of details, 'small acts of cunning' (p. 139) which work as mundane but inescapable technologies for the 'modernisation' and 'transformation' of the whole public sector. Audits of various sorts work 'both to evaluate and to shape the performance of the auditee in three dimensions: economy, efficiency and effectiveness' (Power, 1994, p. 34). The first-order effect of performativity in education is to reorient pedagogical and scholarly activities towards those which are likely to have a positive impact on measurable performance outcomes for the group, for the institution and increasingly for the nation, and as such is a deflection of attention away from aspects of social, emotional or moral development that have no immediate measurable performative value. Watson (2003) asserts that the language of neo-liberalism is 'unable to convey any human emotion, including the most basic ones such as happiness, greed, envy, love or lust' (quoted in Davies, 2005, p. 1). A second-order effect is that for many teachers this changes the way in which they experience their work and the satisfactions they get from it – their sense of moral purpose and of responsibility for their students is distorted. Practice can come to be experienced as inauthentic and alienating. Commitments are sacrificed for impression. The force and brute logic of performance are hard to avoid. To do so, in one sense at least, means letting ourselves down, and letting down our colleagues and our institution. And there is a particular set of skills to be acquired here – skills of presentation and of inflation, making the most of ourselves and making a spectacle of ourselves. Social structures and social relations are replaced by informational structures. The point is that we make ourselves calculable rather than memorable. This is a commodification of the public professional.

Performativity also makes a crucial contribution to the work of metaexchange – the reflexive design and redesign of markets 'by modifying their operation and articulation' (Jessop, 2002, p. 241). The rendition of teaching and learning into calculabilities generates market information for choosers, enables the state to 'pick off' poor performers, and makes it possible to translate educational work, of all kinds, into contracts articulated as performance delivery, which can then be opened to 'tender' and thus to competition from private providers by means of 'contracting out' – a move to metaheterarchy. Contracts bring about a reshaping of the culture and structures of governance (both institutional and national) and of service relationships and of the commitments of public service workers. At heart this is a process of disaggregation and individualization both of governance itself and of service relationships which are increasingly 'conceived as a series of cascading contracts linking principals and agents' (Yeatman, 1996, p. 285). Collectivist conceptions of 'genuinely public values' (Yeatman, 1996) are potentially displaced. The social contract within which the professional works, in the public interest, is replaced by commercial relationships between educator and client and employer. The body politic is replaced by what Foucault (1979, p. 194) calls 'mercantile society', which 'is represented as a contractual association of isolated juridical subjects'. Contractualism and juridical forms are being extended into many aspects of the educational process. Indeed this is a key component of the knowledge economy, or what Lyotard (1984) calls 'the mercantilization of knowledge' (p. 51). Knowledge is no longer legitimated through 'grand narratives of speculation and emancipation' (p. 38) but, rather, within the pragmatics of 'optimization' – the creation of skills or of profit rather than ideals. This is summed up in Lyotard's terms in a shift from the questions 'Is it true?' and 'Is it just?' to 'Is it useful, saleable, efficient?' What is to count as worthwhile knowledge is determined by its 'impact' – this has fundamental implications for higher education research (see for example Ball, 2010b; Slaughter & Leslie, 1997). There is a complex and very profoundly 'effective' set of relationships embedded in all of this. Relationships between the mundane measurements of outcomes in the everyday life of schools, the new forms of managing society and its populations – through the use of 'governing knowledge' – and the interests of capital, as we will go on to explore in later chapters.

We can also think of these processes as a form of what Harvey (2005, p. 159) calls 'accumulation by dispossession', by which he means the redistribution of public or commonly held assets and resources, through privatization and financialization, as private property. This has the effect of fragmenting and particularlising social conflicts (p. 178). Here collective professional values are displaced by commercial values, and teachers are dispossessed of their expertise and judgement. Collective interests are replaced by competitive relations and it becomes increasingly difficult to mobilise workers around issues of general significance to the education system as a whole.

More broadly, Ozga (2008) has been mapping and analysing the increased use, across a variety of European states, of what she calls 'governing knowledge', that is knowledge of a new kind – a regime of numbers – that constitutes a 'resource through which surveillance can be exercised' (2008, p. 264). That is, the use of performance information of various kinds as 'a resource for comparison' (p. 267), addressed to improvements in quality and efficiency, by making nations, schools and students 'legible' (p. 268). These 'numbers' are deployed within schemes like PISA, national evaluation systems, school performance tables, test comparisons, throughput indicators and so on (Rinne, Kallo & Hokka, 2004). These numbers are increasingly important in the ways that states monitor, steer and reform their education systems by the use of targets, benchmarks, and performance-triggered interventions. That is, 'the technology of statistics creates the capacity to relate to reality as a field of government' (Hunter, 1996, p. 154).

The shaping of policy through data and the constant comparison for improvement against competition has come to be the standard by which public systems are judged. Indeed, public systems of education are recreated, and Europe is formed. The mediation of travelling policies and policy discourses across Europe constitutes a polymorphic policy-scape in which quality assurance and evaluation (QAE) has become a major instrument.

(Grek, Lawn, Lingard & Varjo, 2009, p. 121)

There is a marked paradox here in that these techniques, which rest upon the granting of greater autonomy and processes of deconcentration within education systems, provide the state with new modes of governing society and the economy and shaping individuals and individual conduct – these are new arts of government!

Leadership and enterprise and organisational redesign

Performativity and governing by numbers are furthermore organised and facilitated by other techniques of organisational redesign. Leadership and distributed leadership in particular is a means of focusing individuals on goals and practices oriented towards organisation 'improvement' or productivity (or income generation) and the raising of system standards, as Elmore's (2009) account makes very clear. That is, leadership is a means of reworking and narrowing the responsibilities of the practitioner by excluding 'extraneous' issues that are not directly connected to performance outcomes. It is, as Elmore describes it, a move from loose to tight coupling, which ties teaching and learning activities in the classroom (or research activities in HE) 'tightly' to group, organisational and national 'productivity':

Creating a new model of distributed leadership consists of two main tasks: 1) describing the ground rules which leaders of various kinds would have to follow in order to engage in large scale improvement; and 2) describing how leaders of various kinds in various roles and positions would share responsibility in a system of large scale improvement.

(Elmore, 2009, p. 19)

In a distributed leadership system the job of leaders is to buffer teachers from extraneous and distracting non-instructional issues so as to create an active arena for engaging and using quality interventions on instructional issues.

(Elmore, 2009, p. 24)

It is important to recognise that 'leadership knowledge' is nested within a broader discursive ensemble of organisational practices and values that together work to transform public sector organisations into 'the enterprise form' – meaning that these organisations come to 'follow principles of economic sustainability and cost-benefit risk-management and adhere to standards of performance that are adjusted to the reality of an all-encompassing market environment' (Shamir, 2008, p. 6). Gunter (2010, p. 7) describes the UK New Labour government (1997–2010) version of school leadership as 'the business model of entrepreneurial transformational leadership'.

In combination with the strictures and technologies of enterprise (see also Chapter 5) and leadership, performativity produces a 'new' professionalism, what Rose (1996, p. 55) describes as a 'reconfiguration of the political salience of expertise, a new way of "responsibilizing" experts in relation to claims upon them other than those of their own criteria of truth and competence'. The arts and skills of enterprise are a generic form of new responsibility which respond to the strictures of performance. They are particular forms of moral agency and disposition for social action which rest upon a taking of 'responsibility'. As Shamir (2008, p. 4) puts it, 'responsibility is the practical master-key of governance'. Within all of this, there is the interpellation of new sorts of actors who have 'appropriate' reflexive moral capacities. There is a dual and linked set of responsibilities embedded here; one for performance (standards, outcomes, ranking, improvement) done by working on and with students or maximising research 'outputs', but sometimes working on and with data itself (fabrication); and the other for efficiency – cost-reduction (replacing expensive labour with cheaper labour), innovation (which can be addressed to costs or to productivity) and entrepreneurship (which can maximise income by increasing recruitment or by generating new income flows). Together these responsibilities are fundamental to the competitive well-being of the organisation. The first is elicited through the sanctions and rewards of performance, at individual and organisational level. The second is elicited through participation in or the visions of 'good' leadership in relation to the financial disciplines of a market environment. In effect 'the framework of relations between individuals and governments is currently undergoing a profound transition' (Tuschling & Engemann, 2006, p. 451). To the extent that these new responsibilities are taken seriously, the social, political and economic goals of the state are reproduced within the commitments, choices and obligations – the conduct that is – of individual actors within public sector institutions. These 'new' professionals act prudentially and innovatively to protect and further the interests of their organisation – to achieve targets, to maximise income and to compete effectively with other providers within the new market-like mechanisms which are inserted into public sector schooling – a process which enacts the 'general neo-liberal drive to ground social relations in the economic rationality of markets' (Shamir, 2008, p. 3). Enterprise is the trope that holds all of this together.

Leadership and enterprise are also a means of interjecting practical innovations and new sensibilities into areas of education policy that are seen as change-resistant and risk-averse. More generally they 'pilot' and disseminate as 'good practice' the conditions (strategic and discursive) for a 'post welfare' education system in which the state contracts and monitors but does not deliver education services – metaheterarchy – thus creating new opportunities for 'profit' for the private sector or social entrepreneurs or voluntary organisations. Through its metagovernance, and the deployment of the technologies of performance, leadership and the market, the state acts as a 'commodifying agent', both rendering education into a commodity and into contractable forms, thereby 'recalibrating institutions' to make them homological with the firm and creating the necessary economic and extra-economic conditions within the public sector within which business can operate. Here the interests of market and state are conjoined.

Regulatory destatization

This chapter has sought to achieve three main things. First, to highlight the difficult relationships between state and market as these are articulated within neo-liberalism as a doctrine and within the political economy of the 'competition state' (Jessop, 2002) and its strategies of accumulation. Second, to suggest some ways in which these difficulties are being resolved, in part, by the reform of the state itself and the move to metaheterarchy. That is, the reconstitution of the role of the state from that of service delivery to a combination of regulation, performance monitoring, contracting and the facilitation of new providers of public services. That is, also, the shift to new conditions of governing, encapsulated in a process that Jessop (2002, p. 199) calls *destatization* – which 'involves redrawing the public–private divide, reallocating tasks, and rearticulating the relationships between organisations and tasks across this divide on whatever territorial scale(s) the state in question acts'. We will focus more directly on issues of territorial rescaling in relation to education policy in Chapters 5 and 6. However, I am not suggesting that the new forms and modalities of the 'competition state' resolve all of the antagonisms between market and state. Neo-liberals are still greatly exercised by and continue to work on the notion of 'limited government' and reductions to the regulatory activities of the state remain a focus of advocacy and policy activity – as the passing reference to the Indian Right to Education Act indicates. As emphasised above, the neo-liberalising of the state is an evolving and contested and uneven process, within and across nation states, and degrees of regulation and *metaheterarchisation* are two of the important dimensions of variation. The third main concern of the chapter has been to demonstrate the translation of neo-liberal or libertarian doctrine into practice, as a curriculum of reform – in two senses. On the one hand, as political practice and advocacy in the organised interests of neo-liberal think tanks and foundations directly and indirectly funded by capital as a global project. Doctrine is made into policy, programmes, and campaigns. I have begun to indicate the complex, connected, reflexive and effective organisation of this project through networks of discourse, influence and money – more examples and more detail are presented in the chapters which follow. On the other hand, doctrine is also rearticulated in a set of techniques of governing, which have the effect of 'modernising' or neo-liberalising the public sector and its institutions. In doing so, and to achieve this end, relationships, value and values, purposes and indicators of self-worth are 'redesigned'. What we do is changed, but more fundamentally, who we are and how we think about what we do are changed. This is brought about in many very specific ways as the policy proposals of neo-liberal advocates are enacted – policies like school choice, vouchers, devolved management, performance management, leadership and contestability (tenders and contracts). The point is, and I will return to this regularly throughout the book, that we need to understand, research and respond to neo-liberalism not as abstract ideas but as a discourse, in the full senses of the word – a set of practices and subjectivities that are realised in 'actually existing' and mundane forms in different settings and locations.

3 Transnational advocacy networks and policy entrepreneurship

Indiana Jones, business and schooling of the poor

This chapter takes up some of the strands of analysis, concepts and issues introduced in the previous chapter and takes them further. Substantively it focuses on the advocacy of 'private schools for the poor' and on the work of a particular very mobile, neo-liberal policy entrepreneur – James Tooley (see http://www.ncl.ac.uk/ecls/staff/profile/james.tooley) – and the advocacy network within which he moves.

James Tooley – policy entrepreneur

> Like a 21st-century Indiana Jones, University of Newcastle professor James Tooley travels to the remotest regions on Earth researching something that many regard as mythical: private, parent-funded schools serving the Third World poor. Government officials from across Africa, India and China repeatedly tell him that such schools do not exist in their countries—often after he has already visited those schools and interviewed their students and teachers.
>
> (http://www.philanthropyroundtable.org/topic/excellence_in_philan-thropy/an_invisible_hand_up, accessed 31 October 2011)

Tooley is a card-carrying Hayekian, an academic, a 'thought-leader' and businessman. His work has won a series of 'prizes' awarded by 'pro-market' think tanks and advocacy groups (see Box 3.1). He directs, serves on the boards, is trustee, published by, speaks at a variety of interconnected 'pro-market' organisations. As we shall see, he has received large grants for his advocacy and business development work, set up his own charity, businesses and schools, and has a variety of relationships with a wide range of governments, multilateral organisations, charity banks and NGOs.

As we shall see, Tooley performs all three of the functions of a policy entrepreneur (Mintrom & Vergari, 1996). He has identified particular educational needs and offers innovative means to satisfy them; he is willing to take financial and emotional risks in pursing change where consequences are uncertain, albeit with very significant financial support from others; and has been able to assemble and coordinate networks of individuals and

---

Box 3.1 James Tooley

James Tooley won the 2006 Templeton Freedom Prize for Excellence in Promoting Liberty in Free-market Solutions to Poverty, presented in Colorado Springs, USA; the 2007 Alexis de Tocqueville Award for the Advancement of Educational Freedom, presented in Warsaw, May; the 2007 National Free Enterprise Award, presented in London, March. In 2010 he won the Sir Antony Fisher International Memorial Award for his book *The Beautiful Tree*, presented in Miami, Florida. He was also Gold Award Winner of the first *Financial Times*/International Finance Corporation 'Private Sector Development Research Paper Competition', presented in Singapore at the IMF/World Bank Annual Governors' Meeting, September 2006. He also created the Education and Training Unit at the Institute of Economic Affairs in London. He is a member of the academic advisory councils for several think tanks, including Reform, Civitas, Institute of Economic Affairs, Taxpayers' Alliance and Globalisation Institute. He is an Adjunct Scholar at the Cato Institute and a thought-leader for School Ventures.[1]

1 '... School Ventures provides information on conditions that make education markets attractive as destinations for private investment... *it* exists to provide better information to help school operators and their domestic and international investors to make smarter investments'. (http://timbuktuchronicles.blogspot.com/2008/03/school-ventures.html, accessed 2 August 2011)

---

organisations, local and transnational, with the capabilities and resources needed to achieve change. His reputation is formidable and his contacts are extensive and cross-sectoral, again as we shall see, and he works with a diverse group of fellow travellers from academia, charity, business and politics. In particular, Pauline Dixon and Sugata Mitra, but also Andrew J. Coulson, Michael Kremer and Ken Donkoh (see Chapter 4) among others. Furthermore, he clearly possesses both 'strategic ability, and tenacity' (Mintrom and Vergari, 1996, p. 424). In all these senses Tooley is a policy entrepreneur *par excellence*. He is a policy traveller, he animates global circuits of policy knowledge, and is a co-constructor of infrastructures that advocate, frame, package and represent policy ideas. He creates, maintains and utilises a wide variety of 'fragile relays, contested locales and fissiparous relationships' (Rose, 1999, p. 51) and is able to create 'swift trust' (McCann, 2011) to achieve policy mobility and transfer. He takes his policy ideas, or perhaps more accurately the authoritative discourses of neo-liberal economics, into influential and exclusive 'global microspaces'. The global compressions of time and space through technology and travel are increasingly important to the possibilities of policy mobility. More than anything, through his writing and speaking, he is a persuasive storyteller who is able to put faces and figures into the neo-liberal imaginary (see *Educating Amartech* and *The Beautiful Tree*). He also produces 'research' to support his arguments and ideas and is adept at eliciting funds for his projects, to make his ideas real. He gets things done! He has been able to make himself an 'expert of truth' (Rose, 1999) and as Larner (2002, p. 671) puts it, through his single, simple solution to the educational problems of the world he has been able to make the 'incommensurable commensurable'. In effect as he moves through networks of policy relations and between 'sites of persuasion', with his 'fellow travellers', he has been able to 'stabilise' a set of 'rationalities, metadiscourses and logics' which are being 'instituted as the basis for action' (Larner & Le Heron, 2002, p. 760) at great pace. However, while Tooley is an extraordinary 'policy actor' and an exemplar of policy mobility, it is important not to glamorise or romanticise his 'policy work' (see McCann, 2011). He is inserted into a highly developed, long-standing, dense and effective neo-liberal advocacy network, within which the Atlas Foundation Freedom Network is a significant generative component, and he has considerable financial backing, as we shall see. Nonetheless, situating Tooley within this network enables us to identify key sites, connections, methods and practices of neo-liberal advocacy and policy mobility.

Mapping advocacy

In this chapter I will attend to some particular examples of the mobility of the rhetorics and discourses and policy ideas that James Tooley articulates, particularly those which advocate school choice and private schooling as solutions to the problem of achieving universal, high-quality primary education in India and Africa. I also want to indicate some of the complex and blurred relationships between advocacy, philanthropy and business within these networks. This involves the mapping of a set of network relations between advocacy groups in the UK and the US and local 'choice' advocates in India and the ideas which flow through them; a further set of network relationships focused on Africa and articulated through new forms of philanthropic engagement with educational problems are explored and discussed in the next chapter. I hope to begin to show how these particular policy networks 'work' and the 'work' they do for neo-liberal capitalism as a supranational project and as a set of local initiatives addressed to political changes and business opportunities. This grounds neo-liberalism in a set of practices and relationships. At a macro level this rearticulates IMF and World Bank orthodoxies for policy in international fora; at the local level it involves working with startup edu-businesses of various sizes, and at the national level it includes working on and against national policies which block or constrain the development of school markets.

I then go on to sketch some of the emerging impacts of local and transnational advocacy on the politics of education and education policy in India and also finally indicate some of the ways in which local and international businesses are taking up the spaces and opportunities created by the advocacy discourse for involvement in educational services delivery. I do not set out here to debate the issues of private schooling or choice – which I have researched extensively in other settings (Ball, 1997a, 1997b, 2001b, 2003a, and so on; Ball, R. Bowe & S. Gewirtz, 1996) – or seek to interrogate the evidence mobilised in the processes of advocacy.

The data here are drawn from secondary sources of various kinds, mostly accessed through internet searches. These included the websites of advocacy groups, business information websites and newspaper reports, as well as blogs, Facebook and Twitter. The range and variety of sources was extensive and it was possible to draw upon multiple sources for virtually all of the examples and events referred to. All are drawn from sources in the public domain and in many instances employ direct quotation from the individuals themselves. The 'method' relies on simple network-mapping techniques (see Chapter 1) and the attempt to identify the capacities of the network actors in terms of relationships, finance, 'research', promotion and publicity, and so on.

The context

In neo-liberal terms India is a relatively late 'liberaliser' – 'policies of structural adjustment and liberalisation were not initiated until the early 1990s. The spread of market relations and discourses has been relatively slow' (Nambissan and Ball, 2010, p. 4). However, in a recent interview Krishna Kumar identifies a clear set of relations between liberalisation, privatisation and modernisation in India and suggests that education has become 'a significant arena to study liberalisation' (LaDousa, 2007) and that 'privatisation has become a major force' (p. 139).

Where education is concerned, India has as yet failed to achieve universal access to elementary education. According to the 2011 UNESCO EFA Monitoring Report (UNESCO, 2011), despite a rapid reduction since the previous review, 5.6m children in India were out of school in 2007 – over half of the world's children out of school live in 15 countries. The report also notes that: 'In some countries, including India, Nigeria and Yemen, the 2004–9 projection points to an increase in out-of school numbers by 2015' (p. 42). This sort of analysis provides fertile ground for the use of forms of 'accountability politics' by private school advocates – holding politicians to account for policy promises and failures.

There is already in India a relatively small but rapidly expanding market in private unregulated elementary schools that are officially 'unrecognised' by the state. This market 'has emerged in response to the growing demand for better quality (English medium) education by lower middle class and poor parents who are willing to pay for this education for their children' (Nambissan and Ball, 2010, p. 4). There is also a stratified market of private and international schools aimed at the middle and ruling classes. Such demand has created 'opportunities' for private investment in elementary education, both in new private school provision for the poor and in the work of 'improving' the quality of state-funded schools (see Chapter 5).

Despite the beginnings of recognition of private schools in the 2009 Right to Education Act (see Chapter 2) the acknowledgement or encouragement of the private market for elementary education for the poor remains politically sensitive and is still met with considerable opposition within the main political parties, although there is considerable political interest and support in some states (particularly Andhra Pradesh – see below). It is only very recently that any statistics on private, 'unregulated' schools have been collected and their existence formally acknowledged. Thus, two of the initial tasks for pro-private/pro-choice 'advocacy groups have been to destabilise the opposition to private provision of schooling, and to bring some credibility to the existing extra-legal (unrecognised) schools' (Nambissan and Ball, 2010, p. 4).

India's 'policy entrepreneurs': articulation and repetition

Within the new politics of education in India there are opportunities for advocacy and business. In particular, neo-liberal policy entrepreneur James Tooley 'has played a key role in building and shaping the school choice discourse in India and he occupies a variety of roles and positions in the networks that link organisations and individuals who are presently pushing the "project" of neoliberalising India's schools' (Nambissan and Ball, 2010, p. 5) (see Figure 3.1). Tooley, a former consultant of the International Finance Corporation,[1] was director of a global study of investment opportunities for private education in developing countries, *The Global Education Industry* (Tooley, 1999), now in its second edition.[2] The Templeton Foundation provided further funding of $US 800,000 for Tooley's comparative study of private schools in five countries, which included an Indian component. One of the sites where the research was undertaken was in one poor district in the city of Hyderabad in the southern Indian state of Andhra Pradesh. One of Tooley's objectives in this research was to show that these private schools were outperforming the public sector schools, that the poor were accessing private schools and that they were willing to pay for education (Nambissan and Ball, 2010, p. 5), and that the private schools are also socially committed (providing free places to the needy). None of this, he felt, was being adequately acknowledged, the 'discovery' of which he describes in *The Beautiful Tree* (Tooley, 2009). The book is published by the 'pro-market' Cato Institute in the USA (see Chapter 2) and by Penguin India, a subsidiary of Pearson Education (see Chapter 6).

I realized that something quite remarkable was going on in the back streets of Hyderabad. It seemed that my expertise in private education

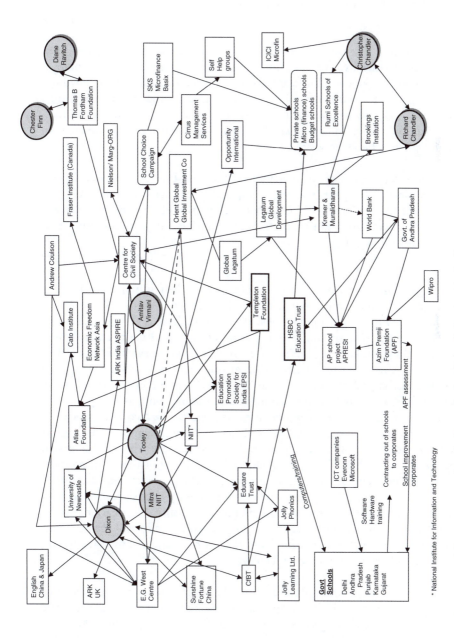

Figure 3.1 Advocacy networks, choice and schooling of the poor in India.

* National Institute for Information and Technology

might have some relevance after all in my urge to help the poor. Clearly, what was happening must have implications for the way we viewed education in developing countries?

(Tooley, 2009, p. 18)

Also, he argues that private schools were making profit and if invested in or supported financially, for instance, with low-cost innovative technology, they would be a potential area for business expansion. Altogether, for-profit schools aimed at poor communities are presented as the solution to India's problems of access to and quality of education and as a lucrative business opportunity. Tooley muses in *The Beautiful Tree*, referring to the teachers in the for-profit schools he visited:

> These teachers seemed pretty good to me. But how would largely untrained, low-paid teachers compare with their trained, well-paid counterparts in the public schools? How would the children achieve under them? As I toured the schools, I realized it was something that I had to find out.
>
> (Tooley, 2009, p. 13)

The importance of such 'findings' is not just in their initial reporting but through their cumulative circulation and reiteration at diverse points of articulation. Pro-market foundations and think tanks and their media play a key role 'in the take up and dissemination of ideas and their establishment within policy-thinking. Using findings from his own research in Hyderabad and West Africa Tooley has been able to reach a wide and varied audience through his books, academic journals' (Nambissan and Ball, 2010, p. 5). He has published versions of his findings in academic journals and they also appear on a huge range of online sites, in reports, in media interviews, a BBC documentary (see http://news.bbc.co.uk/1/hi/programmes/newsnight/ 4631175.stm), as well as in the many lectures and talks that he has given, including to parliamentarians (US and UK) and policy-makers and political groups in India and around the world at networking events (see Chapter 4). As noted above, in 2006 James Tooley won an essay competition sponsored by the *Financial Times* and the International Finance Corporation, and a prize of $30,000, for his essay *Educating Amaretech*, also called the 'Gold Essay' based on his IFC and Templeton funded research.[3] Andrew J. Coulson of the Cato Institute reported of Tooley:

> His work leapt into high gear in 2002, after a fortuitous meeting in Goa, India, with Templeton Foundation senior vice president Charles Harper. Impressed with Tooley's study of private schools in the impoverished Old City section of Hyderabad, Harper encouraged him to draft a proposal for expanding his investigations on an international scale. ... The result was a Templeton Foundation grant of nearly

$800,000, allowing Tooley and his colleague Pauline Dixon to compare government and independent schools in Ghana, Nigeria, Kenya, India and China. Their conclusion? It is better to give students and their parents a hand up than a handout—and that the hand up should come from Adam Smith's 'Invisible Hand,' the free market.

(Center for Educational Freedom, accessed 14 June 2011)

The essay is a good example of what Keck and Sikkink (1998) call 'symbolic politics', which involves the use of stories or symbols which make sense of advocacy claims for distant audiences (Nambissan and Ball, 2010, p. 6). There has been extensive media coverage of Tooley's exploits (particularly among 'pro-market' newspapers and magazines and websites). For example, the Philanthropy Roundtable reported:

... in every region he studied, private school students were outscoring their government-sector counterparts in both mathematics and English, a language recognized in these countries as a valuable economic asset. The effect was both statistically significant and large in real terms, and persisted even after controlling for student background characteristics and IQ. Private schools were doing this, he added, for a small fraction of the per-pupil expenditures in the public sector. Fees at the private schools he studied in Hyderabad hovered around $2 per month, and at least 18 percent of students in these schools attended for free or at discounted rates—the poor were subsidizing the truly destitute.... As the messenger of such shocking, anti-establishment findings, Tooley did what any good scientist would do: He requested the reanalysis of his data by a respected independent body—the British National Foundation for Education Research. After a thorough review of his Hyderabad data, using the latest statistical methods for assessing educational outcomes, NFER agreed with Tooley's findings—except that they found the private sector advantage to be even greater than his original estimate....
(Philanthropy Roundtable website: http://www.philanthropyroundtable.
org/printarticle.asp?article=1479, accessed 2 April 2011)

Almost all of the US, UK and Indian foundations and think tanks which have drawn attention to and disseminated Tooley's work are related and interconnected through the Atlas Economic Research Foundation's Liberty Network. Tooley's writings about his private school projects or features on his work have also been published by: the Hoover Institution; the Fraser Institute (and he is consultant to the Institute's School Chain Showcase, http://www.fraserinstitute.org/programs-initiatives/school-chain-showcase.aspx); the Mackinac Center; the Institute of Economic Affairs (of which Tooley is a member); the Adam Smith Institute; and the National Center for Policy Analysis. In India his work has also been reported by the School Choice Campaign, India – its slogan is 'Fund Students, Not

Schools!', and the campaign features on the website of the Atlas Economic Research Foundation. It also appears in *Policy*, which is published by the Centre for Independent Studies, the *UNESCO Courier*, and publications of Opportunity International, India Together, The Educare Trust and the Liberty Institute[4] and was presented at the Mont Pelerin Society[5] regional meeting in Goa. Tooley's paper 'The Enterprise of Education. Opportunities and Challenges for India' has been published by the Liberty Institute[6] (also part of the Liberty Network). Through these 'sites' and their relationships there is a continual reappearance and rearticulation and relegitimisation of advocacy 'knowledge'. Papers like Tooley and Dixon (2005), 'Private Education is Good for the Poor: a study of private schools serving the poor in low-income countries' (Washington DC: Cato Institute); and 'Teacher Absence in India: A Snapshot', by Kremer, Muralidharan, Chaudhury, Hammer and Rogers (*Journal of the European Economic Association* 3 (2–3): 658–67, 2005), and other work by Tooley's collaborator Pauline Dixon (see below), acquire the status of baseline truth as they are quoted time and time again as evidence of state failure and market successes.

Local nodes and education business

In India the key sites for school choice and privatization advocacy are the Liberty Institute, the School Choice Campaign India, which is run by the Centre for Civil Society, and the Educare Trust (still in reference to Figure 3.1). However, 'increasingly school choice/private schooling advocacy networks also include investment companies and venture capitalists that are looking to new market opportunities' (Nambissan and Ball, 2010, p. 6) (see Chapter 4, 'Enterprising schools'). Tooley argues that: 'Crucially, because the private schools serving the poor are businesses, making a reasonable profit, they provide a pioneering way forward for investors to get involved too' and that 'investing in a chain of schools – either through a dedicated education investment fund or through joint ventures with educational entrepreneurs – could help solve the information problem for poor' (2005, p. 1). He further argues that 'brand reliability' would provide market information to poor choosers. In 'Educating Amaretech' Tooley also cites Prahlad's observation (the founder of the Aravind Eye Care System, which provides cataract surgery for large numbers of the poor in India), that he was 'inspired by the hamburger chain, McDonald's, where a consistent quality of hamburgers and French fries worldwide results from a deeply understood and standardised chemical process' (Prahlad,[7] cited in Tooley, 2005, p. 9, see note 3). According to Tooley, 'there is every reason to think that a similarly "deeply understood and standardised" learning process could become part of an equally successful model of private school provision, serving huge numbers of the poor' (2005, p. 9) (Nambissan and Ball, 2010, p. 7). Further, since private entrepreneurs already provide 'free and subsidized places for the poorest, sensitively-applied targeted vouchers could extend access with equity on a large scale' (ibid). He also argues that microcredit can be used to fund small entrepreneurs to 'start up' micro-schools that will give them an adequate return on their investment (see below).

Another idea floated by Tooley is the setting up of Education Quality Zones (EQZs) which would have 'more relaxed rules and regulations regarding education' along the lines of the Economic Priority Zones (EPZ) that have been established by the Indian Government 'to foster entrepreneurship and innovation'.[8] Similarly, some leaders of the Indian business community have also called for 'setting up special education zones' to free education from 'the control of bureaucracies and regulating bodies'.[9] Both the 'roll-back' and 'roll-out' phases of neo-liberalism are evident here, the pressure for a smaller, more modest, limited state, a relaxation of state regulation, and an expansive and freer market in educational services.

In 2007 Tooley received a further financial boost to his work in India when the 'philanthropic arm' of Orient Global, a Singapore-based investment firm run by New Zealander Richard Chandler, established an education fund of $100 million. Chandler is reported to have created the fund as a result of reading Tooley's article 'Low-cost schools in poor nations seek investors' in the *Financial Times* (17 September 2006). Tooley is President of the Fund and its main purpose is to target for investment the private school market for children from low-income families in India. Coulson (2007) reports that the education fund 'will follow a three-pronged strategy: invest in publicly listed and private enterprises that will further its mission while helping to sustain it over time (for example, the Fund has acquired a 9.4 per cent stake in India's NIIT educational chain); conduct research and development for a pilot chain of budget private schools for the poor in India; and make grants to existing private schools to aid in their expansion and protect them from sudden political or economic shocks'. Kalra (2007), writing in the online newspaper *Mint*, quotes Tooley as saying 'We have started looking at investment opportunities in private schools running in slums ...', and goes on to say that 'Tooley did not disclose details of his business model, but said he was exploring tie-ups with microfinance providers, such as Hyderabad's SKS Microfinance and Basix, to offer loans to entrepreneurs who wish to open schools in low-income areas'[10] (Nambissan and Ball, 2010, p. 7) (see below on Microfinance).

There are two other international PEs in the Indian school choice/private schooling advocacy network who work closely with Tooley. They are Pauline Dixon and Sugata Mitra. Dixon is Director of Research at the E. G. West Centre at the University of Newcastle. Her doctoral degree, awarded in 2003, was for her work on 'The Regulation of Private Schools for Low-Income Families in Andhra Pradesh, India: An Austrian Economic Approach'. She was International Research Co-ordinator in the Templeton Project (2003–5) directed by Tooley. She has written and published with

Tooley and a number of her publications focus on her work in India.[11] She has co-authored (with Tooley) a chapter on private education and the poor for the 2006 *Index of Economic Freedom*, published by The Heritage Foundation and *Wall Street Journal*[12]. She was teacher and writer of the course 'Educational Freedom: A Global Perspective', which was a winner of the Freedom Project, managed by the Atlas Economic Freedom Foundation and funded by the John Templeton Foundation.[13] Dixon has also been invited by Capitol Hill, the Heritage and Templeton Foundations and the Cato Institute to speak on her research on private schooling for the poor, and has been associated with a project funded by the Centre for British Teachers (CfBT), *Private Schools for the Poor* (2001–2). Dixon worked for the Orient Global Project (2007–9) where she was a Project leader, along with Tooley and Mitra, and is the joint author, with Tooley, of the *Pearson Handbook on Educational Management* chapter on 'budget private schools'. In 2003 she won the Don Lavoie essay prize (he was a Hayekian economist based at the Cato Institute), which is run by the Society for the Development of Austrian Economics, for her paper about private schools in India, and she has been a speaker at the European Center of Austrian Economics Foundation. She also undertook a policy review of the regulation of private schools for the Centre for Civil Society. She has also worked with Tooley in Ghana, Nigeria and China and is involved with Tooley's Chinese education company Sunshine Fortune. She is also involved in ARK's[14] (Absolute Return for Kids) ASPIRE programme in India (Sally Morgan, Paul Marshall, Amitav Virmani and Charles Abani, all of ARK (see Ball & Junemann, 2012), appear in her blog pages), and is associated with the promotion of the teaching of reading by phonics in India and China, through the Jolly Phonics (Susie and Flavia Jolly and http://www.rrf.org.uk/pdf/nl/53.pdf) and the Genki English companies (in Japan and China) (http://www.genkienglish.net/start.htm) (run by Richard Graham). Amitav Virmani, ARK's Director of Programmes in India, was a lead speaker at the School Choice National Conference 2010: The Right to Education Act: Revolutionary, Redundant, or Regressive? run by the School Choice Campaign, which is the CCS's flagship project (see below). Here again we can see the joining up of ideas which move through and are reiterated by think tanks, advocacy groups, academic institutes and companies.

Mitra, the so-called Slumdog Professor (after the film *Slumdog Millionaire*, http://www.guardian.co.uk/education/2009/mar/03/professor-sugata-mitra), was a research scientist with the National Institute for Information and Technology (NIIT). He received accolades for his 'Hole in the Wall' (HIW)/ 'minimally invasive education' and is hailed on Edutopia (What works in Public Education) (an information gateway run by the George Lucas Educational Foundation) as the 'Inventor of the off-the-wall idea for Hole-in-the-Wall Education: Put a free computer workstation in the wall of a poor New Delhi neighborhood, and the local children will quickly learn to use it through their own curiosity and experimentation'.[15] Mitra was named by the George Lucas Educational Foundation as one of the 'Global Six of 2007'.

> Like the film, Mitra's educational initiatives have also beaten all expectations. Delhi now has 48 computer 'holes', and Mitra – who has taught educational technology on master's courses at Newcastle University for the past two years – is expanding his project to UK primary schools, using the same techniques to help children in Gateshead as he used in Hyderabad, India.
>
> (http://www.guardian.co.uk/education/2009/mar/03/
> professor-sugata-mitra)

Mitra argues that the HIW education is more effective and far cheaper than government schooling and can be aimed at and serve the needs of the poor. With backing from the ICICI Bank (see below) and IFC-founded 'Hole-in-the-Wall Education', Mitra and NIIT set up 250 computers in 110 locations throughout India and later in Cambodia. Mitra asserts that test results indicated that on a computer skills test HIW students performed almost as well as formally educated students: 'and their engagement and performance in school improved as well'. Tooley, in his lectures and writings on education for the poor, often refers to Mitra's low-cost HIW technology. Mitra is now Professor of Educational Technology at the University of Newcastle and he 'aims to spread this model around the world to boost the learning and life skills of children, particularly those living in poverty and with few educational resources'.[16]

In all of this I am trying to illustrate the dense international and local connectivity which is social as well as political and businesslike and which links philanthropies (ARK etc.), think tanks (CATO etc.), businesses (NIIT, Global Orient, Jolly Phonics – http://www.focusonphonics.co.uk/acatalog/ phonic_ph-readingschemes_jollyphonics.html etc.), advocacy groups (Centre for Civil Society, Reading Reform Foundation etc.), academic research and policy ideas – demonstrating the strength of (variably) 'weak ties'. We also glimpse here some of the sinews of a network which is also a discursive and epistemic community underpinned by versions of libertarian economic theory. There also are relationships and connections between different sorts of 'right-thinking' policies like choice and vouchers, and phonics, and entrepreneurial schools. These connections are indicated by the actors themselves through their websites and blogs, Facebook and Twitter (see Chapter 4), through which seamless narratives of policy possibilities and policy successes are constructed and disseminated and 'site visits' are photographed and reported (http://blogs.ncl.ac.uk/pauline.dixon?blog=559& page=1&disp=posts&paged=6, accessed 26 January 2011) and remade as 'actionable' ideas (McCann, 2011).

The network(s) here is very much a social community, with elements both durable and fleeting, held together by 'meetingness' (Urry, 2003) – galas, receptions, conferences, and policy tourism – a particular kind of policy lifestyle. They have depth and complexity, only some of which is 'visible' – but which can be 'seen' in the photographs on blogs – they are full of overlaps, recurrences, multiple relationships. The form and content of relationships are enormously diverse and multifaceted and not easy to classify. There is a mix of lasting ties and episodic collaborations and intricate interdependencies which link local projects to international relations which provide expertise, reputation and legitimisation. The networks join up and maintain the epistemic policy community, which is bound together by the concepts of 'freedom' and 'choice', through local ties and exogenous connections. While 'he' does not explain or account for the networks, Tooley is a key nomadic, rhizomatic connector (Rizvi & Lingard, 2011).

These networks constantly evolve and are generative and dynamic (see Chapter 4); new sites, outlets, and opportunities are constantly being spawned and created within network relations, with the effect of building social capital. Again, this proliferation works to extend the flow of ideas and multiply positions from which to speak and create the appearance of widening acceptance. Specific idiolects develop which are shared across the sites and speakers (see below). Network members publish each other's work, speak at each other's events and find funding for each other's projects – reiteration rather than openness. Within all of this, there are some new kinds of careers – 'ideas careers' – based on a kind of self-making (Beck, 1992, p. 55). Novel ideas (or repackaged old ideas) are traded through advisory or consultant positions, or through projects or publications. The people with ideas come to represent and sometimes enact their ideas. They are what Stone (2000) calls 'knowledge actors'. Also, 'straddling' and boundary spanning is important – movement between different sectors and fields. One of the defining characteristics of many of the key participants in policy networks is their ability to move between social, political and business worlds – they practice what they preach by breaching traditional boundaries and by being flexible and adaptable.

Choice and schooling: local organisations and advocacy

A number of local organisations have emerged in the last few years in India with the express objective of promoting school choice and private schooling for the poor. Foremost amongst them is the Centre for Civil Society (CCS). As well as the Liberty Network, CCS is a member of Economic Freedom Network Asia (EFNA), which is linked to the Fraser Institute and the Liberal Institute of the Friedrich Naumann Foundation in Berlin (see Figure 3.1 for networks linking intellectual entrepreneurs and advocacy organisations). It presents itself as a 'think tank' which is concerned with ideas and says: ' ... we don't run primary schools, or health clinics, or garbage collection programs. We do it differently: we try to change people's ideas, opinions, mode of thinking by research, seminars, and publications. We champion limited government, rule of law, free trade, and individual rights. We are an ideas organisation, a think tank that develops ideas to better the world'.[17] Tooley is a Senior Research Fellow with CCS.[18] Its mission is 'Building a campaign for school choice in India. The need to create a discourse on choice in education, state the case for private schooling among the poor and giving poor parents the freedom to choose'. The case for 'deregulation and delicensing of private schools, legalizing for-profit schools, and microfinance and venture capital for budget private schools' is stressed. The website goes on to say that 'Today it is virtually impossible to start a legally recognised school. Also, since many of the schools for the poor are unrecognised, they cannot get a bank loan to improve their infrastructure like any other enterprise'. CCS deploys research evidence to bolster its case. Tooley's Hyderabad research and Eva Weidrich's essay 'Vouchers: Is there a Model for India?' can be downloaded from the CSS website (Weidrich, 2007).[19] Tooley has also undertaken a study of the access to private schooling among poor families in settlements in East Delhi for CCS along the lines of his Hyderabad study, and come up with similar findings.[20] The study was supported by the Goodrich, Thomas B. Fordham and Templeton Foundations. More recently a CCS survey, 'Education for the Poor', was carried out by market research companies AC Nielsen and ORG-MARG, Delhi (Nambissan and Ball, 2010, p. 10). The study 'tried to gauge customer satisfaction with government school education'.

The CCS 'School Choice Campaign' was launched in January 2007. As a part of the campaign, vouchers were to be awarded to poor children in seven states.

> In Delhi, applications were invited from parents in poor settlements and around 400 children were chosen through a lottery. The vouchers worth up to INR 6000 were awarded at a venue frequented by the cultural elite of the city and was reported by the media. Significantly, the chief minister of Delhi state was present to give away the vouchers. The CCS web site appeals to prospective donors in India, UK and US to contribute to the voucher fund and has also forms for donations posted on the web site.[21]
>
> (Nambissan and Ball, 2010, p. 10)

The CCS claims that the response to the campaign has been 'overwhelming', their 'biggest support is from dalit and tribal activists', and that it is 'gaining ground in Bihar, Delhi, Jharkhand, Orissa, Tamil Nadu, Uttar Pradesh and West Bengal'. CCS goes on to say 'Most people realise that the aspirations of the poor are no different from us and they too want their children to attend English medium private schools which will lift them out of their present poverty and give them a decent future. Also, the moment the poor become a bit less poor, they escape the system of government schools'. The 'campaign' is being managed by a private management company, Cirrus Management Services (CMS), which is taking it to states where the organisation has links with community-based organisations built around microfinance loan programmes, involving banks like SKS (see below). 'Ashok of Cirrus says that his organisation "hand-holds" self-help groups in seven States including Tamil Nadu, and has decided to leverage its reach to start a voucher programme'. He goes on to say that they are 'working with a group of individuals and corporates to develop and finance private schools across rural India, initially across 700-plus villages, to be scaled up subsequently' (Nambissan and Ball, 2010, p. 11).[22] Cherubal, a CCS vice president, observes that 'for the voucher programs to be widely available, the government has to embrace them, or the idea will not scale. . . . If Pilot projects are started in every state, the Government could use them as examples to consolidate and ultimately take over the voucher scheme'.

The Educare Trust (ET) is a 'non-profit agency' and was registered in 2002 by James Tooley together with 'other members associated with private unaided schools' under the Indian Trust Act, 1882.[23] Tooley's Templeton-funded study (2003–5) was based at the Trust. The Director of the Trust, Gomati, had worked with Tooley previously on a CfBT project also focused on private schools for the poor and he later worked on the Templeton project. The Trust has also taken part in research relating to the use of Jolly Phonics for the 'improvement of English literacy teaching in private unaided schools' as a component of the Templeton project involving Pauline Dixon, who is the International Adviser to ET. The Trust also has a 'marketing manager' who is involved in the marketing of the 'Jolly Phonics English Literacy Programme' and computer programs along with Sugata Mitra (ET website). The Trust also runs a microfinance programme,[24] microfinance loans are extended to private schools, and has a scholarship fund called the EG West Scholarships which is to 'help economically deprived children in rural and urban India to pursue education in private unaided schools'. The Trust website reports that 'more than 300 children are currently benefiting from the support of the Educare Trust. Professor E. G. West was a renowned British educationalist, who conducted research on private education as a vehicle for helping the poor to help themselves, in Britain, the USA and developing countries. The scholarships are named in memory of his enduring influence'.[25] As noted already, James Tooley is Director, and Pauline Dixon Director of Research, of the E. G. West Centre at the University of Newcastle.

AP school choice project

One of the main tasks that the Indian pro-choice advocates have set for themselves is to demonstrate that children involved in the voucher programmes and attending private schools perform better than their peers in government schools. In addition to Tooley's research, a study began in 2009 in Andhra Pradesh that seeks to do this. This is the Andhra Pradesh Randomized Evaluation Study (APRESt). APRESt was initiated by Karthik Muralidharan, an assistant professor of economics at the University of California, San Diego and Venkatesh Sundararaman, a senior economist at the World Bank, in partnership with the Azim Premji Foundation (APF), which is the philanthropic arm of the corporate giant Wipro and is closely involved in government initiatives to improve primary education outcomes. The study is supported by a number of other organisations and individuals and reflects the interests that inform the spread of private markets in education in India,[26] including the World Bank (see Figure 3.1). One part of the project aims to 'pilot alternative policy options to improve rural primary education and rigorously measure their impact in rural areas of Andhra Pradesh'. The partners have signed a Memorandum of Understanding: 'to continue to pilot and rigorously evaluate (using randomized allocation of programs) the most promising options in primary education policy over a period of 5 years under the APRESt' (Nambissan and Ball, 2010, p. 12).

The education components of the APRESt design have two elements. One offers scholarships to poor children 'to shift to schools of their choice (if they wish to) in addition to the option of continuing in the existing government school. Such a program would provide opportunities for children from disadvantaged families to attend private schools. The research study involves a rigorous evaluation of the impact of school choice both on children who receive the choice as well as on the aggregate impact on education outcomes for all children in villages where the school choice program is implemented....'. The other is introducing and evaluating the impact of performance-related pay for teachers in the rural schools. The lead financial partner for the project Legatum Global Development funds both the scholarships, covering the full cost of tuition for 6,000 children in 100 villages, and the evaluation of the study[27] (see Box 3.2). The project will be evaluated by Kremer[28] and Muralidharan, the authors of the teacher absenteeism study mentioned earlier and both are CCS 'School Choice Scholars', and Sundaram of the World Bank. APF, the Government of Andhra Pradesh (GOAP) and the World Bank will be 'instrumental in ... helping the results feed into the policy process through the institutionalization of APRESt in GOAP's education program' (ET website). APRESt is one of a cluster of projects and interventions around choice and private schooling, each of which adds to and reconfigures the 'plumbing' (Grabher, 2004, p. 114) or ecology of existing networks and network knowledge.

Again what is striking here is the recurrences and overlaps, cross-referencing and multiple roles and the political work of advocacy. Business, banking, philanthropy, multilateral agencies, state governments and advocacy networks are mobilised around research and innovative programmes by a set of common interests and a common cause. The work of the Indian advocates is also taken up by and related to and through other international networks, nodes and points of articulation and dissemination,

---

Box 3.2 The Legatum Foundation

Legatum Global Development is part of The Legatum Foundation. The Legatum Foundation provides humanitarian grants to support community-based projects run by local entrepreneurs in the sectors of health, education, economic empowerment, human liberty, disaster recovery and the environment. The Legatum Foundation is funded by Legatum Capital, which is a privately owned, international investment organisation or hedge fund, with its headquarters in Dubai. Legatum's primary focus is commercial investment, and it has applied its expertise and investment to a long-standing involvement in the sustainable development of communities around the globe. The company invests in the ICICI and HDFC banks in India, and owns a controlling share of Microfin, India's largest microfinance institution. Legatum Capital is headed by Christopher Chandler, who also founded the Legatum Center for Development and Entrepreneurship at MIT, which sponsors students from developing countries who aspire to launch businesses back home. In 2009 he was 701st on the Forbes Magazine billionaires list. He is brother and one-time partner of Richard Chandler, Head of Orient Global Investments, which finances the Global Orient Fund, and who was 307th in 2010 on the Forbes Magazine billionaires list, with a net worth of $3.1bn. Richard also awards the 'Freedom to Create' prize and funds a chain of schools in India, of which James Tooley is Chairman – the Rumi Schools of Excellence (http://www.rumieducation.com/our-schools.html). The Enterprising Schools website (see Chapter 4) describes Rumi Education as 'India's first chain of truly affordable private schools' and says, 'Parents choose our schools for a quality education that costs just Rs. 150-400 per month ... Rumi Schools of Excellence established operations in Hyderabad in March 2008 with nine foundation schools serving 4,000 children. Working with existing private schools, we are able to improve the quality of education delivered to each child by providing talented school entrepreneurs with a portfolio of education services ...'

(various website sources)

---

like for instance: Enterprising schools, Beyond profit, Opportunity International (to which we will attend below and in the next chapter). The setting up of and 'success' of projects in one location serve as models and legitimacy for initiatives in other settings.

In this respect the focus of a good deal of private school and reform activity in Andhra Pradesh and Hyderabad needs underlining. Hyderabad has recently and quickly emerged as a hub of the global information technology economy; Kamat (2011, p. 197) argues that 'Hyderabad illustrates the socio-political and historical context that transitions the developmental state into a "competition state" in which the state subordinates the welfare and developmental needs of its citizens in favor of the profitability of the corporate sector and political elites'. Kamat sees the 'visionary' and charismatic leadership of Chief Minister Naidu and his proposal to create HITEC City (Hyderabad Information Technology Engineering Consultancy City), as an example of 'actually existing neoliberalism': 'Andhra Pradesh and its capital city offers a unique narrative of neoliberal globalization and resistances to it, at the same time that it represents an exemplary case of the neoliberal project' (Kamat, 2011, p. 190). The political leadership of Andhra Pradesh and its projects and the 'synergy between education/economy that have configured Hyderabad as an island of growth amidst a region of immiseration and underdevelopment' (Kamat, 2011, p. 194) created a 'policy window' opportunity which was conducive to the development of private school initiatives. In part these initiatives are facilitated, as noted above, by microfinance loans – which are a major vehicle for recent charity banking and venture philanthropy activity (see Stewart et al., 2011) around the globe. In India, microfinance has shifted from a charitable to a commercial sector of operations. In Andhra Pradesh in particular, microfinance has become big business, with banks like SKS, Microfin, ICICI, Basix and Axis building up large portfolios of small loans. These microfinance banks have become attractive to international equity investors (e.g. ICICI and Microfin – Christopher Chandler/Legatum Capital and SKS – George Soros). The Indian School Finance company (ISFC), founded by Gray Ghost Ventures (see Chapter 4), also specialises in small loans to edupreneurs, and is a member of the Enterprising Schools network; S. Viswanatha Prasad, formerly of Basix Bank, and Brajesh Mishra, formerly of ICICI Bank, are board members of ISFC.

> We provide loans to private schools at the lower end of the pyramid to unlock their dreams that have been constrained on account of lack of capital. ... With ISFC taking care of the money problems, the schools can focus on improving their schools and the quality of teaching, thereby positively impacting the lives of millions of children for years to come.
>
> (http://www.isfc.in/)

Here again, there are actors who move between education, advocacy and finance; as noted earlier, Richard Chandler has established the Rumi Schools of Excellence, in which Tooley is also involved. Representatives of Basix and SKS have been involved in School Choice Campaign events, and SKS, through its SKS Educational Society, has established the Bodhi Academy schools. However, the microfinance sector in Andhra Pradesh has recently gone into crisis, with charges of overselling and increasing repayment defaults. SKS has been particularly hard hit and in November 2010 received financial support from other banks including ICICI and Axis, and Christopher Chandler's Microfin has delayed its IPO. The AP government has imposed new restrictions on microloans and following a series of suicides by microloan borrowers 100 microfinance agents, including two Microfin managers, were arrested.

> The financial sector crisis in Andhra Pradesh seems to be playing out like a very bad dream that doesn't end. It has been 33 days since the State Government of Andhra Pradesh passed a sweeping Ordinance governing all lending activities in the state by banks as well as non-bank finance companies (with only perhaps State Bank of India excluded from its ambit since it is not constituted as a company under the Companies Act but through its own Act) with stipulations that no collateral may be taken, repayments must be monthly, nobody must have more than one loan outstanding, all financial services business must be carried out in government offices and the permission of government agencies must be taken before any loans can be taken.
>
> (http://indiamicrofinance.com/andhra-pradesh-microfinance-crisis-indian-mfi-822030u6.html, accessed 14 June 2011)

Microfinance and microschools

Opportunity International was founded in 1971 and was one of the first microcredit lenders, offering small business loans, savings, insurance and training in basic business practices to women and men living in chronic poverty.

> Opportunity International provides small loans – sometimes as little as $50 – and other services that allow poor entrepreneurs to start or expand a business, develop a steady income, provide for their families and create jobs for their neighbours.
>
> (Opportunity International website)

The Opportunity International website quotes James Tooley as saying: 'I am thrilled that Opportunity International is expanding schools for the poor. I have seen the benefit that these schools bring to an entire community – the parents, the families and especially the children who are getting a quality education from teachers who are dedicated and committed'.[29] (See Box 3.3.) In turn, Opportunity International refer to Tooley's research to legitimate their loan programme.

Crane (CEO, Opportunity International) says 'Microschools are usually located right in the neighborhoods where the poor are concentrated. ... As a result, parents tell us they feel safer sending their daughters to these schools.

Box 3.3 Opportunity International

Opportunity International launches Microschools™ – new frontier in breaking the chain of poverty

New research shows 'schools for the poor' outperform public schools in developing world

Opportunity International, a leading innovator in the microfinance industry, today announced the expansion of its microfinance school loans program to bring greater educational opportunity to poor children, especially girls. Microschools of Opportunity™ is a new initiative that provides loans to 'edupreneurs' who open schools in poor neighborhoods where children cannot access public school for a variety of reasons.

Groundbreaking research by James Tooley, a leading academic expert on schools for the poor, has shown that these schools outperform their public school counterparts across Africa, India and China. Tooley's research provided inspiration for the development of Opportunity International's new microschools™ program.... 'Microschools of Opportunity is the third leg of the stool to help the poor escape poverty and transform their lives once and for all,' said Christopher A. Crane, president and CEO of Opportunity International.

(Opportunity International website)

This will help break the discriminatory cycle that has existed against girls in many poor countries.'[30]

The HSBC Education Trust and the Centre for British Teachers (CfBT – a very profitable not-for-profit, see Chapter 4) are also involved in microfinance-microschool advocacy in India. In 2004 the CfBT[31] launched a project called EQUIP (Enabling Quality Improvement Programmes in Schools) that will facilitate private schools to get microfinance from HSBC. CfBT will take a lead role in 'identifying schools on the basis of an evaluation of the potential of the school for improvement ... Schools that are approved by CfBT will receive loans for infrastructure ... These schools will have to take a CfBT-designed School Improvement Plan ... and the progress will be monitored through an Education Management Information System'.[32] The loans ranged from Rs. 50,000 to Rs. 5,00,000. The project aimed to enable government-recognised private schools that admitted children of low-income families to get financial aid from the bank to improve their infrastructure. This was in the nature of a 'pilot project, to be implemented in Andhra Pradesh and Tamil Nadu' and 'later be rolled out across the country'. *Business Line* (19 July 2004) reported that 'about

30 private schools in the city have shown interest in joining the initiative. Of them, 16 will be given loans in the first phase'. The Minister for School Education of the AP Government was also quoted as asking HSBC 'to expand the scheme to government schools that form more than 80 per cent of the 91,000 schools in the State'[33] (Nambissan and Ball, 2010, p. 14).

The microfinancing of private schools has also generated business for companies offering advisory services to 'start-ups'. One such is Intellecap, which is also involved in the APRESt project. Intellecap was set up in 2007 with equity investment from Global Legatum and also offers support for the setting up of private school franchises. It appears on the Enterprising Schools website (http://enterprisingschools.com/blogs/scaling-low-cost-profit-education-provision-franchise-way, accessed 29 April 2011).

Three sets of entrepreneurship come together, overlap and interrelate here. There is policy entrepreneurship, as outlined above, the 'selling' of policy ideas; edupreneurship, as represented in the creation of individual and chains of lost-cost private schools; and microfinance, which links between the two as a form of funding for 'start-up' school enterprises. As we shall see in the following chapter, venture philanthropy and venture capital are also both interested in investment in the low-cost private school market.

The state, public private partnerships, sponsorship, philanthropy and government schools

The final strand in this complex story of money, ideas and politics in India concerns Public Private Partnerships and the other business interests that they indicate, and the role of business philanthropy. The language of Public Private Partnerships (PPP) began to appear in education policy documents in India in the late 1990s when corporate organisations expressed their interest in participating in efforts towards EFA. CCS advocates PPPs on its website. In particular, information technology is seen by some policy makers in India as the panacea for improvement of the quality of education in state-funded schools and a means of addressing the aspirations of poor parents (Nambissan and Ball, 2010, p. 14) and through PPPs in education, a number of IT companies have become involved in schools (see Box 3.4). NIIT is a nodal player in the growth of the state school education business (see box). This is Sugata Mitra's parent organisation, and a major player in educational software development; as noted, the Orient Global Fund is a major investor.

A number of state governments have entered into agreements with companies like NIIT to supply and maintain computer networks and train students and teachers in their use. The official website of the government of Punjab State declares that it is

> encouraging the participation of private sector for providing good quality education by giving a package of incentives in the form of land

Box 3.4 IT in schools and business

Everonn Education Ltd. provides computer education services to eight state governments in India. It has so far trained about 1.2 million students and has set up about 1900 computer laboratories. The company educates students from schools and colleges on a contractual basis. Recently, the company signed a Memorandum of Understanding with Gujarat Council of Primary Education to train 5,400 teachers. It will implement computer-aided learning in about 1,250 schools in the state. This is a system using a computer and LCD projector via a VSAT receiver, through which a single instructor is able to teach hundreds of students all over the country at the same time. Everonn has managed to spread its operations to ten states (including Tamil Nadu and Pondicherry).

One of the leading educational companies in India, Everonn is listed in both the NSE and BSE. It recently opened a chain of private schools – KenBridge Schools – and in 2009 launched a charitable trust, the Everonn India Foundation, 'to uphold the company's commitment towards spreading quality education across rural India' (Everonn website).

NIIT also has a presence in 2,000 Government schools in the states of Andhra Pradesh, Tamil Nadu, West Bengal and Karnataka.[1]

1 Edited from: http://www.theindiastreet.com/2007/07/introduction-everonn-systems-india.html (10 July 2007).

at cheaper rates along with other facilities. The Punjab State Government has proposed to set up a chain of *Adarsh Schools*, at least one in each Block, for providing high quality education even at village level ... Every school is allowed to lease out spare land to the private contractors, for cultivation. The income so received from this is spent on the development of the respective school.[34]

The Confederation of Indian Industry (CII) is also involved in initiatives (along with Coca Cola India, Bank of America, Honda Siel etc.) for 'quality improvement' of education for poor children in slums in Delhi. It is said to have 'facilitated linkages between the State Government and Member Companies for IT-Enabled Education (which may merely mean bringing computers to schools/training teachers to use them). It has helped in the signing of an MOU between Microsoft and the Municipal Corporation of Delhi (MCD) for training teachers at 1,000 MCD schools in Delhi' (Nambissan and Ball, 2010, p. 15). 'The idea is to empower the teachers to use IT as a tool for classroom teaching'.[35] The market for IT in schools is large and growing and the policy climate is encouraging the participation of businesses in state schooling as a way of 'improving' the quality of education.

A number of Indian corporations (like Everonn) have set up 'philan-thropic' foundations which have education as part of their remit. There is a range of corporate effort, especially at the elementary stage, and private participation in government-run schools 'in the provision of infrastruct-ure and facilities, the supply of mid-day meals as well as involvement in the development of curriculum, pedagogy and assessment and in the provision of computers and software as well as technical support and training. Foundations established by corporate houses such as the APF (Wipro) and Pratham (ICICI) are an increasingly visible presence in the arenas of education policy making and in initiatives aimed at quality improvement in government schools in some States' (Nambissan and Ball, 2010, p. 15).

More recently, some state governments have begun to contract out 'underperforming' schools to philanthropies and corporate foundations. The Bharati Foundation, which is funded by the mobile phone company Air Tel, will be running fifty government schools in Rajasthan as part of a School Improvement Programme and has a goal of establishing 1,000 Satya Bharati schools across India. The *Akshara Foundation*, a Bangalore-based Public Charitable Trust with the mission to provide education for children of the poor, was established in the year 2000 by the wife of the CEO of Infosys, a company which 'designs and delivers technology-enabled business solutions for Global 2000 companies' (company website). The Foundation has a range of programmes that provide 'multiple solutions for univer-salizing elementary education' (company website) and is 'a part of the Pratham Education Initiative and has replicated Pratham's approach of comprehensive, scalable, replicable and cost-effective education solutions' (see Chapter 4).

Discussion

The Indian choice and privatisation advocacy network (Figure 3.1) is con-nected by a complex of funding, exchange, cross-referencing, dissemination, and mutual sponsorship – the latter involving various aspects of what Keck and Sikkink (1998) call 'information politics'. The Centre for Civil Society, the Educare Trust, EPSI and the Liberty Institute (member of the IPN and Liberty Network; its CEO won the Sir Antony Fisher Memorial Award in 2001) are key points of the local articulation and flow of the choice policy ideas but are also engaged directly or indirectly in a bigger enterprise of neo-liberal state reform and the redefinition of the boundaries of the policy process – policy channels are being diversified.[36] As the website of the Liberty Institute puts it: 'The Institute particularly seeks to improve our understanding of market processes; to identify the factors that may have restricted the evolution of the market and ways of overcoming those factors;

to estimate the costs – social and economic – of curbs on the market forces; to propose market-based alternatives to government regulations in the economy'.[37]

The Indian pro-choice think tanks are also linked to other co-belief organisations in other countries in a worldwide advocacy network for neo-liberal ideas. This is a formidable network of power, influence, ideas and money which presents a simple message easily understood by politicians and policy-makers in diverse locations. The work of this TAN follows very clearly Brenner and Theodore's (2002) conception of two distinct but dialectical moments in the dissemination of neo-liberalism; that is, critique, and attempts to change public perception of policy issues, followed by the 'creation of a new infrastructure for market-oriented, economic growth, commodification, and the rule of capital' (p. 364). Government education policy and government schools are subject to sustained critique, often on the basis of 'research' evidence (research and evaluations are locked within closed circles created by the privatisers and their allies); alongside this, new educational opportunities are being created for some sections of the poor in India, while at the same time new opportunities are being opened up for small and big business, both in terms of the creation of a business infrastructure for private education and pressure for legal changes to enable private for-profit schooling and vouchers. The Indian state is vulnerable in this area of policy given its 'failures' around universal provision and EFA goals and is therefore very susceptible to the politics of a TAN that is very well funded and backed by a variety of powerful and influential voices, local and transnational. The shared libertarian values of the network members are a key resource in all of this. The activities of this TAN are interacting with and expanding the discursive and policy spaces within which educational businesses, voluntary organisations and charities can flourish – supported by commercial and philanthropic microfinance and multinational investment. These discourses also seek to expand the range of policy choices available to the Indian government and naturalise within Indian politics key neo-liberal technologies, including contracting out and public–private partnerships.

This network constitutes an 'epistemic community' organised around a mutually recognised set of 'knowledge' issues (Grabher, 2004, p. 111), baseline truths and a 'vision' (see Box 3.5), which are continually rearticulated and circulated. This is a 'particular type of persuasive story-telling, involving strategic namings and framings, inserted into a specific context where actors are predisposed to a certain range of policy options ...' (McCann, 2011, p. 23). Nonetheless, these ideas are made powerful and influential by money, effective relationships and action on the ground. They provide expression for political and business interests. These are, at the same time, *ideoscapes* and *financescapes*, that is, big ideas and commercial infrastructures, to use Appadurai's (2006) terms. They are part of the complex geography of neo-liberalism which extends into and beyond the nation state

Box 3.5 EasyLearn schools

Welcome to EasyLearn, Class 1

The unions are scaremongering. The present reforms are only toying with privatisation. To bring profit and fees into that system – now, that would be progress. What could it look like here? Gazing into my crystal ball, I see chains of learning centres carrying the distinctive bright orange logo of 'easy learn' competing with those sporting the red 'V' of 'VirginOpportunity'. Competition between these players would make good schooling affordable to all, accelerate the pace of learning innovation, and end the system mired in complacency and underperformance. I guess the unions would be right to be worried then. But parents and children could rest easy, and grasp the new opportunities offered.

(James Tooley, *Times Online*, 17 April 2006)

and make its imaginary real. The actors involved work to 'transfer, emplace and utilize certain forms of knowledge as part of their practice' (McCann, 2011, p. 15). It renders policy mobilities into embodied practices.

Another way of thinking about Tooley and his activities in India and elsewhere is that he is a latter-day missionary seeking to convert ineffective state education systems to the church of enterprise. That is, as a paternalist, neo-colonialist, he is dispensing Western ways of thinking, naming and solving the problems of post-colonial societies, and ultimately opening up new forms of exploitation and dependency in the form of profit for multi-national edu-business. However, Tooley makes the point that he 'discovered' entrepreneurial schools already at work in places like Hyderabad and Lagos, and in India at least claims to be restoring or reinventing a pre-colonial form of indigenous schooling. Furthermore, he sees scope for the West to learn from these developments.

What is important in the work of this TAN is that the concern and focus on India, especially as far as James Tooley is concerned, is not merely because of the potential for profitable markets in schooling for poor children but that these developments will generate evidence and political support which demonstrate to the West that 'for-profit' education can work – and 'if India can do it so can we', leading to a reassessment of the role of the state in education in Western countries. The E. G. West Centre website has Tooley arguing this quite clearly:

Certainly stories of the educational entrepreneurs in the slums, battling against hostile government and real poverty, can provide inspiration to the school choice movement in the West. But I also think it can provide more than that ... What the West did for the school choice debate in the 1960s and 1970's, the evidence from India and elsewhere can do for the school choice debate now: if the evidence reveals the poorest worldwide achieving better educational outcomes without the state, then this must help inspire and buttress appeals for increased school choice in rich countries now. It also raises anew the question: what is government doing in education at all.[38]

This was reiterated by Tooley on the Outlook Business website (23 August 2008), where he asserts that 'a silent revolution is brewing in low-cost private school chains. In the next wave, they might even "colonise" the West'. We need to think about the 'flow out' of Western political and business ideas and their 'flow back'!

Notes

1 The World Bank has had more than a decade of close association with state run primary education in India through the Bank-supported District Primary Education Programme (DPEP).
2 See website: http://www.ncl.ac.uk/ecls/staff/profile/james.tooley.
3 James Tooley (2005) 'Educating Amaretech: Private Schools for the Poor and the New Frontier for Investors', in *Economic Affairs,* Vol. 27, No. 2, pp. 37–43, 2007.
4 The Liberty Institute was established in 1996 in Delhi, India, as a 'non-profit organisation'. It sees itself as 'an independent think tank' dedicated to 'empowering the people by harnessing the power of the market' and declares that 'We seek to uphold the four institutional pillars of a free society – Individual Rights, Rule of Law, Limited Government and Free Market' (http/www.libertyindia.org).
5 The Mont Pelerin Society is an international organisation composed of economists (including eight winners of the Nobel Memorial Prize in Economic Sciences), philosophers, historians, intellectuals, business leaders, and others who favour classical liberalism. Its founders include Friedrich Hayek, Karl Popper, Ludwig von Mises, George Stigler and Milton Friedman. The society advocates freedom of expression, free-market economic policies, and the political values of an open society.
6 Tooley, James (2001) 'The Enterprise of Education. Opportunities and Challenges for India', *Liberty Institute Occasional Paper* no. 6. Available online: http://www.libertyindia.org/publications.htm.
7 Prahlad is known as the advocate of the BOP or 'bottom of the pyramid' thesis, which he elaborates in his book: Prahlad, C. K. (2004) *The Fortune at the Bottom of the Pyramid: Eradicating Poverty Through Profit.* Upper Saddle River, NJ, Wharton School Publishing.
8 Eva Weidrich (2007) 'Education Vouchers: Is there a Model for India?', available on the CCS website: http://www.ccsindia.org/policy/ed/studies/wp0072.pdf.

9 http://news.education4india.com/2037/nasscom-chief-for-setting-up-special-education-zones.

10 Kalra, Alpana (2007) 'Education Bulletin: Education Fund Eyes Pvt Schooling for the Poor', in *Mint,* http://schoolchoice.in/campaign/newsroom/20070517.php (17 May 2007).

11 See http://www.ncl.ac.uk/egwest for a list of publications.

12 psdblog.worldbank.org/psdblog/2006/01/index_of_econom.html (accessed 24 March 2009).

13 Ibid.

14 ARK see Ball 2011 and http://video.moglik.com/v/rUlIGs0mvto/ARK-ASPIRE-Programme.htm.

15 Rubenstein, Grace (2007) 'Sugata Mitra – Catalyst of Curiosity', http://www.edutopia.org/sugata-mitra.

16 Ibid. – for all quotes on/by Mitra.

17 See: http:// www.ccsindia.org. Quotes are from the CCS website.

18 http://www.ccsindia.org/ccsindia/Newsletter/feb-mar07.htm. J. Tooley, K. Muralidharan, A. Coulson and M. Kremer are also mentioned as School Choice Scholars, see http://www.schoolchoice.in/choice/index.php.

19 Weidrich, op. cit.

20 See James Tooley and Pauline Dixon, 'Private Schools Serving the Poor' 5, Working Paper, CCS.

21 http://schoolchoice.in/campaign/support/fund_vouchers.php.

22 Ibid. for details and quotes.

23 See www.educaretrust-India.org/about.html.

24 Ibid. for all quotes.

25 http://www.educaretrust-india.org/research.html.

26 Details about the project and quotes are from 'Andhra Pradesh School Choice Project Proposal', see http://siteresources.worldbank.org/EDUCATION/Resources/278200–1121703274255/1439264–1178054414297/karthikmuralidharan.pdf.

27 Legatum Global Development is an 'international private investment organsiation' and 'part of the Legatum group of companies that has been investing in the world's capital markets for over 20 years and whose mission is to create a legacy of enduring investment success, while applying the same principles of effective capital allocation to promote sustainable human development'. http://www.legatum.org/about.htm.

28 Michael Robert Kremer is a development economist and is currently the Gates Professor of Developing Societies at Harvard University. He is a Fellow of the American Academy of Arts and Sciences, a recipient of a MacArthur Fellowship and a Presidential Faculty Fellowship, and was named a Young Global Leader by the World Economic Forum. Kremer is also a Research Affiliate at Innovations for Poverty Action, a research organisation based in New Haven, Connecticut dedicated to creating and evaluating solutions to social and international development problems, and is a senior fellow at the Brookings Institution and writes for the Independent Institute. He is also founder and president of WorldTeach, a Harvard-based organisation which places college students and recent graduates as volunteer teachers on summer and year-long programmes in developing countries around the world.

29 www.opportunity.org/NETCOMMUNITY/Page.aspx?pid=410&srcid=265.

30 www.opportunity.org.
31 CfBT Education Trust is a leading education consultancy and service organisation. We provide education for public benefit both in the UK and internationally. Established 40 years ago CfBT Education Trust now has an annual turnover exceeding £100 million and employs more than 2,500 staff worldwide who support educational reform, teach, advise, research and train. Since we were founded, we have worked in more than 40 countries around the world, including the UK, managing large government contracts and providing education services as well as managing directly a growing number of schools. We are a not-for-profit organisation (registered charity – number: 270901). (Website accessed 2 August 2011.)
32 See http://www.hindu.com/2004/07/20/stories/2004072014360300.htm (20 July 2004).
33 http://www.thehindubusinessline.com/2004/07/20/stories/2004072001511900. htm (20 July 2004).
34 See http://punjabgovt.nic.in/education/GovernmentPolicy.htm (downloaded on 10 May 2008).
35 http://www.indianamericancouncil.org/afc/education.htm (downloaded on 10 May 2008).
36 The global networks in which these local organisations are situated carry other concomitant discursive baggage, including conservative religious ideology (e.g. Templeton Foundation and Opportunity International), anti-statism, anti-welfare, radical forms of liberty, the 'enterprise narrative' and in some cases, anti-global warming stances.
37 www.libertyindia.org/about.htm (accessed 24 March 2009).
38 E.G. West webpage.

4 'New' philanthropy, social capitalism and education policy

Again here I want to pick up some themes, loose ends and starting points from the previous chapter. Specifically, I will explore the role of philanthropy, or more precisely 'new philanthropy', and 'social capitalism' in fostering and promoting 'market-based solutions' to 'wicked' social and educational problems, and indicate some of the ways in which this fits within and fosters the neo-liberal imaginary. 'New philanthropy' and 'social capitalism' are explained below. I will also look a little more closely at the means and methods of networking within new global policy networks.

Particular attention will be given to the work of the Clinton Global Initiative and other fora and events – occasioned activities – and virtual groupings, as new sites of policy mobilization and 'globalising microspaces'. These sites, events and activities, or 'moments of encounter' (Amin & Thrift, 2002, p. 30), and the social networks which join them up, operate between and beyond traditionally defined arenas of policy formulation, such as localities, regions and nations – on a different scale and in different spaces. As illustrated in the previous chapter, neo-liberal policy narratives and policy advocacy are founded within vibrant global social, political and financial relations which are maintained and extended virtually through email, Facebook, Twitter and blogs (see Box 4.1) but these relationships also have to be 'activated' and 're-embedded', they have 'to be performed, they have to come together from time to time especially to talk' (Urry, 2004, p. 1). So here there is a dual focus on spaces and places, movement and fixity, immediacy and history, the virtual and the embodied, the stable and the fragile. However, as the chapter progresses I will try to use the distinction between space and place in a different way; as suggested by Rizvi and Lingard (2010, p. 66), 'It is interesting to contemplate the significance of a conceptualization of the space of policy production and the place of policy implementation …'. That is, I will 'follow the money' involved in one example of a for-profit, low-cost, private school initiative.

This will extend the sort of analysis begun in the previous chapter by rendering the neo-liberal imaginary into a set of specific, located and embodied practices, both as policy and as business and philanthropy, rather

Box 4.1 Tooley's tweets

Jan 2007 'Talk in Milan.'

Aug 2007 'On my way to New Zealand to give the Annual John Graham Lecture, in Auckland Thursday and early next week in Christchurch.'

Sept 2007 'Coming back from LSE gig with Michael Kremer.'

April 2009 'Rather hot and humid in Mumbai, where I'm judging a social entrepreneur competition.'

May 2009 'Working with Ken Donkoh, Omega Schools, setting up a chain of low cost private schools in poor areas near Accra, Ghana.'

June 2009 'On way to Lagos, to be lead speaker at the 2nd Education Summit.'

June 2009 'Sitting on stage with the deputy governor of Lagos State terrific. We need vouchers and charter schools for Lagos.'

Sept 2009 'Writing a proposal to study low cost private education in Sierra Leone.'

Oct 2009 'In Hyderabad for the Affordable Private Schools Symposium. Great initiative from Gray Matters Capital.'

Oct 2009 'Terrific conference in Washington DC. Jeb Bush is a wonderful guy, full of great ideas on education.'

July 2010 'First to Ghana. Omega Schools doing well, nearly 4,500 students and opening four new schools for September.'

(Accessed at http://twitter.com/#!/jnt007, 3 August 2011)

than as an abstract juggernaut of ideas. I will draw initially on McCann's (2011) work on the international mobility of housing policies, in two ways. First, by looking at some policy nodes and sites of persuasion – meetings, seminars, symposia, workshops, forums and conferences – in which policy ideas and narratives are 'continually enacted, performed and practiced' (McCann, 2011, p. 27) and 'are then assembled into a set of "actionable" ideas' (p. 31). Second, by pursuing further the exploits of a policy entrepreneur and network 'driver' (Dicken et al., 2001), James Tooley. The aim here is to explore and develop:

> A methodological lens that focuses simultaneously on specific sites and on global forces, connections and imaginaries and reflects a concern with how to theorise the relationships between fixity and mobility, or territoriality and relationality, in the context of geographies of policy.
>
> (McCann, 2011, p. 43)

Policy mobilities

This chapter and the previous one begin to outline an ethnographic biography of James Tooley – not a hagiography I hope. This is not done with the object of romanticizing or celebrating him or his work, but rather with the purpose of using him as both a symbol and a medium of the dissemination and realisation of the neo-liberal imaginary. By focusing on some of his activities, relationships and communications it becomes possible to trace, map and 'see' how policies move in the global interstices – beyond states. Some glimpses of the movements (Milan, Hyderabad, Lagos, Mumbai, New Zealand, Washington) and interconnections here are given in Box 4.1.

In this very small sample of tweets we see examples of policy entrepreneurship (the conferences, summits, meetings, research), social relationships (Kremer – see Chapter 3, Bush, Donkoh, State minister of Education, Lagos) and organisations (LSE, Omega Schools, Gray Capital, Affordable schools – see below). These glimpses again indicate the sense of social and epistemic interconnectivity and the density of the networks across which Tooley and his peers move. This is networking as well as a network. Actors move between nodes and occasioned activities and trace a cartography of belief and advocacy. Again this is a generative network, evolving by recruiting adherents and persuading gatekeepers. The joining up of epistemic, financial and policy endeavours is exemplified by the Annual John Graham Lecture 2010 (funded by DBB Capital Merchant Bankers) ... 'Grounds for hope: the irrepressible success of community-led education for the poor', which was given by James Tooley at the Maxim Institute. The Maxim Institute is a politically conservative, New Zealand think tank with a primary focus in the areas of education, family, justice and welfare issues. The Maxim Institute has received several international think tank awards from the Atlas Economic Research Foundation (see Chapter 3); The Templeton Freedom Prizes were awarded to Maxim for: Institute Excellence (first place), Social Entrepreneurship (second place) and Initiative in Public Relations (second place). In April 2006, the Atlas Foundation named the Maxim Institute's *Parent Factor* publication as the winner of the Innovative Projects category of the Sir Antony Fisher International Memorial Award (see Chapter 2).

Policy ideas do not move in a vacuum, they are social and political creations that are told and retold in policy microspaces. They are 'shaped and given momentum in the telling of stories during meetings' (McCann, 2011, p. 32). In these microspaces, powerpoints are presented, documents are circulated, videos shown, experiences recounted, 'research' is reported, and policy successes celebrated in processes of 'contingent, cumulative, and emergent knowledge production' (McCann, 2011, p. 36). Again some of this cumulation can be glimpsed in Tooley's tweets. These policy microspaces are pre-eminently social settings and events of speaking and exchange where trust is built, commitments are made and deals done. 'Trust between people ... gets worked at, involving a joint performance by those who are deemed to be "in the conversation"' (Urry, 2004, p. 12). Participants trade upon and develop various forms of social and network capital which translate into the right to speak and the necessity of being heard. As we shall see, two forms of sociality intertwine; the sociality of meaning and the sociality of wealth.

I will look at a couple of these sites of speaking and exchange in some detail again later, as in previous chapters, to examine the relationships involved – 'the connective social tissue' (McCann, 2011, p. 28) – the activities entailed and the discourses which circulate. James Tooley reappears in some new places and guises. I will also seek once again to indicate the interconnections and overlap between sites. The issues of microfinance and charity banking re-emerge here and will be given further attention; in relation to these the roles of social enterprise, 'social capitalism' and 'social purpose' companies will be discussed. Let us begin with 'new philanthropy'.

New philanthropy or philanthropy 3.0: silver bullets and grand challenges

> New philanthropy is hands on and strategic. New philanthropists will expect to see a 'return' on their 'donation'. This is sometimes also called *Philanthrocapitalism* (*Economist*, February 2006) that is the idea that charity needs to start to resemble a capitalist economy in which benefactors become consumers of social investment. 'This is an integrating business approach to spur an entrepreneurial spirit for the welfare of humankind.'
>
> (http://observer.bard.edu/articles/opinions/216)

What is 'new' in 'new philanthropy' is the direct relation of 'giving' to 'outcomes' and the direct involvement of givers in philanthropic action and policy communities. That is, a move from palliative to developmental giving.

> They're watching the next generation of wealthy donors direct their money to causes and charities that differ from those of their parents and grandparents. In many cases, there is also a shifting of dollars away from large established charities to smaller ones that allow donors to better see how each dollar is spent and measure the results. 'This is philanthropy 3.0,' said philanthropist Charles Bronfman of the Seagram liquor empire, at a recent roundtable discussion with eight philanthropists, in their 20s and 30s, at his Philanthropies' offices in Manhattan.
>
> (http://blogs.wsj.com/financial-adviser/2010/03/08/
> not-your-parents-philanthropy, accessed 3 August 2011)

Handy goes further to describe what he calls 'new new philanthropy' – that is:

> Hedge fund and private equity managers who via their own founda-
> tions, choose to 'invest' their donations in other charities and projects
> and use the latest money-market strategies, research tools and techni-
> ques to manage the performance of their portfolios.
> (http://www.managementtoday.co.uk/news/741088/
> the-new-new-philanthropists, accessed 31 October 2011)

These new sensibilities of giving have led to increasing use of commercial
and enterprise models of practice as a new generic form of philanthropic
organisation, practice and language – venture philanthropy, philanthropic
portfolios, due diligence, entrepreneurial solutions, and so on. The 'new'
philanthropists want to see clear and measurable impacts and outcomes
from their 'investments' of time and money.[1] In this way the business perspective is brought to bear upon social and educational issues and problems.
This is indicative of a generic shift within business philanthropy towards
forms of strategic and developmental philanthropy based on the methods of
private equity investment, a particular mix of caring and calculation, or as
Bronfman and Solomon (2009)[2] put it in the subtitle of their book *The Art
of Giving*, this is where 'The soul meets a business plan'. New philanthropy
also involves the deployment of business strategies and methods, particularly
those of venture capitalism, in relation to social problems by the funding of
innovative and sometimes 'risky' solutions to 'wicked' social problems.
Funders will normally expect to see a 'return' on their 'donation' but accept
that some risky 'investments' will fail. The new crop of philanthropists
is looking to do more with less. They are focusing on smaller start-up
organisations and looking for ways to leverage their gifts. Venture philanthropy, or Philanthropy 3.0, is founded on three working principles:
'bringing non-profits to scale' by committing large blocks of funding over
long periods of time; emphasising evaluation and performance management;
and fostering 'investor–investee' relations on the basis of 'consultative
engagement'.

> To us, social innovation is about much more than philanthropy and
> we've evolved our programs from beyond just donations. We believe
> in philanthropy 3.0 – the idea of moving beyond purely monetary
> contributions and taking a holistic approach that includes the involve-
> ment of our partners, and the donation of our services and technology
> expertise to provide one comprehensive solution.
> (Hewlett Packard's Gabi Zedlmayer, vice president of global social
> innovation, quoted in HP's corporate blog – http://h30507.www3.hp.
> com/t5/Data-Central/Philanthropy-3–0-HP-s-Gabi-Zedlmayer-
> Discusses-New-Approaches-to/ba-p/89223)

These approaches to giving form the basis of what are sometimes called 'silver bullet' solutions and are being aimed at what are called 'grand challenges'. Silver bullet solutions (see: http://www.alliancemagazine.org/en/content/community-foundations-silver-bullet-or-just-part-answer) have three components; they are technical (usually based on the application of a single, new technology), they are generic (that is, universally applicable, irrespective of the diversity of local contexts), and they are scalable (amenable to 'scaling up' from local to national and even international levels). The 'affordable private schools' discussed in the previous chapter and below are a good example. The 'grand challenge' is more recent and takes the idea of the silver bullet further in directly addressing the goal-driven development agenda, like the Millenium Development Goals, and again appeals to a new generation of private philanthropists seeking to apply business methods to 'strategic' giving – that is, problem-focused, inter-disciplinary, time-limited, 'high impact'. The focus is on 'extending leverage' through fostering collaboration – and convergence – between the public and private sectors. Grand Challenge solutions involve the use of 'all tools, all the methods, of financing social change' (Wales, in Brilliant, Wales & Rodin, 2007, pp. 3–4).

> The support given to the grand challenge approach to research and development by a new generation of philanthropists, led by the BMGF [Bill and Melinda Gates Foundation], has played a significant role in promoting a 'logic model' for philanthropy linking ideas about change, leverage and scale in a particular way. Edwards (2008) has identified this phenomenon as 'philanthrocapitalism'; characterised by a belief in the benefits of transferring business methods to the social sector, 'extending leverage' by linking with the private sector, and rapidly 'going to scale', thus maximising returns on investment. These developments draw on two pre-existing trends; 'venture philanthropy' and social enterprise. Key to the latter is the principle of 'blending' the values and contributions of different sectors, so that the Foundations' traditional role of 'correcting for' the market is transformed to one of 'connecting to' the market.
>
> (Brooks, Leach, Lucas & Millstone, 2009, p. 4)

Traditional lines and demarcations, public and private, market and state, are being breached and blended in all of this and are no longer useful analytically as free-standing descriptors.

> We are now officially in the era of 'phylantrepreneurs' where the difference between a VC [venture capital] fund and a foundation, a hot start-up and social venture become totally blurry.
>
> (http://marmoogle.blogspot.com/2007/04/global-philanthropy-forum-that-is.html)

The Bill and Melinda Gates Foundation (BMGF), now the largest private foundation in the US, is the model for 'Philanthropy 3.0' and the brand leader in silver bullet and grand challenge philanthropy (see Kovacs, 2010 for detailed analyses of BMGF). In 2005 it had an endowment of $28.8 billion, a figure that was doubled overnight in 2006, when Warren Buffet announced that he would donate the great majority of his fortune to the Foundation.

Through CSR programmes, corporate foundations and individual philanthropic action, wealthy families and rich companies are beginning to 'assume socio-moral duties that were heretofore assigned to civil society organizations, governmental entities and state agencies' (Shamir, 2008, p. 9; Brooks et al., 2009). These new methods and commitments create new opportunities for those with money and purpose in what Horne (2002) calls the 'parapolitical sphere'. That is, as Frumkin (2006, p. 1) argues; 'philanthropy allows private actors to act in public ways' or as Saltman (2010) puts it more directly, givers 'vote with their dollars'.

The Clinton Global Initiative

One specific arena where grand challenges and silver bullets are very much in evidence is the Clinton Global Initiative (CGI). The Clinton Global Initiative was founded in 2005 by former US President Bill Clinton. CGI is a non-partisan organisation that convenes global leaders to devise and implement innovative solutions to the world's most pressing problems. Each year, CGI hosts an Annual Meeting in September, scheduled to coincide with the UN General Assembly. The BMGF are major funders and supporters of the Clinton Global Initiative and Bill Gates has spoken at CGI forums. The BMGF and Google jointly sponsored the first CGI conference. High-profile CGI events bring together the rich and powerful, ranging from Angelina Jolie to Rupert Murdoch, all eager to 'do good' and to do what Breeze (2007) calls 'identity-work'.

On its own terms, the CGI brings together a set of international policy actors and groups operating at different levels and on different scales towards a single end. In particular, it provides an infrastructure for and brokering of new solutions to educational problems (health, sustainability and gender equity are other more prominent areas of focus) and initiates new policy networks through which ideology, ideas and discourse flow. It constructs and animates new *epistemic policy* communities focused on the application of market-based solutions to social problems.

> Traditional approaches to aid are not enough to address the great global challenges of our time. Market-based solutions show incredible promise to solve these daunting problems on a systemic and widespread level. These approaches, however, are still in a nascent stage. Corporations are researching and developing better business practices that meet social

and environmental bottom lines while producing profits. Non-profits are pioneering enterprise-based models that offer potential for long-term sustainability. Governments are contributing their resources to encourage and support market-based approaches. At the 2010 Annual Meeting, members will discuss the best strategies for bringing these solutions to scale, so the benefits can be felt by more of the four billion people who subsist on less than $3 a day.

(http://www.clintonglobalinitiative.org/ourmeetings/2010/
meeting_annual_actionareas.asp?Section=OurMeetings&
PageTitle=Actions%20Areas, accessed 25 August 2010)

The CGI works by brokering 'commitments' between states, funders and providers and by 2010 had 'garnered' 1,950 such commitments, valued at $63bn, and established partnerships in 170 countries. CGI claims that because of the efforts of its members 'more than 110 million children have gained access to better education' and '650,000 people have learned new professional skills' (CGI website).

Two specific examples of education 'commitments' will give some indication of the nature of the activities and relationships that are produced within and around the CGI. These examples will also be used as the focus of more specific education policy networks in order to 'fill in' the obligations, exchanges and interactions that activate and deliver the 'commitments'. These networks also illustrate the strengths and weaknesses of the network 'method'. They provide a way of 'seeing' the history, infrastructure and ensemble of ideas that underpin 'market-based solutions' – social enterprise, entrepreneurship, 'doing good by doing well' – that make social investment possible and make it work. However, it is not possible here, for very simple practical reasons, to, as Dicken et al. argue, trace the networks to their 'end' (see Chapter 1 and Ball & Junemann, 2012). The narratives of the 'commitments' are culled and constructed from a variety or websites, reports, press releases and so on, and should be read with that in mind. The language used, methods described and claims made are interesting in themselves but there is no evidence at this time for the success or otherwise of the initiatives, apart from self claims and partisan accounts. Some of the sums invested vary between reports, and some websites quoted are themselves sites of advocacy; I have tried to cross-check information whenever possible.

Bridge International Academies (BIA)

Bridge International Academies is a for-profit business founded in 2000 by Jay Kimmelman, Phil Frei and Shannon May. Kimmelman was founder and CEO of Edusoft, an assessment management platform developed to service the measurement and benchmarking requirements of No Child Left Behind (see Burch, 2009), which was sold to Houghton Mifflin in

2003 for an undisclosed sum, but valued at $20m. In an article in the
African Technology Development Forum Journal (2009), James Tooley notes that:
'Three years ago, I began advocating that investors and entrepreneurs
should set up chains of low cost private schools. Jay Kimmelman came to
visit me and my team in Newcastle and then went to Kenya to set up
NewGlobeSchools' (http://www.atdforum.org/IMG/pdf_ATDF_Journal_De-
cember_ 2009_V6_ I1_2.pdf, accessed 3 August 2011).

The 2008 CGI Forum produced a 'commitment' from Deutsche Bank
Americas Foundation ($150,000), the Kellogg Foundation and Gray Matters
Capital (see below) to fund New Globe Schools to develop a chain of 200
schools in Kenya and India. New Globe Schools quickly became Bridge
International Academies and in the 2009 CGI forum Bridge obtained a
further investment of $1.8 million from the Omidyar Network 'to bring
high-quality, low-cost education to Africa'. The Omidyar Network, which
describe themselves as a 'philanthropic investment firm' and as 'investees in
action', is funded by Pierre Omidyar, billionaire founder of eBay, 'and wife
Pam based on their conviction that every person has the power to make a
difference' (company website).

> In January 2010, Bridge International will open five affordable schools
> in Nairobi, educating more than 1,000 new students next year. Bridge
> International also announced Matt Bannick, Managing Partner at
> Omidyar Network, will join the board. With Omidyar Network's
> investment, Bridge International will rapidly increase access to high-
> quality affordable education to poor families across Africa, said Jay
> Kimmelman, Bridge International's Co-Founder and CEO.
>
> On average, children in Africa perform at the 3rd percentile
> academically compared to children from developed countries. Bridge
> International works to close this gap through a network of outstanding-
> quality schools that nonetheless cost less than $4/month per student.
>
> (Omidyar website)

By the end of 2009 Bridge International Academies had raised a total of
$4.35 million from international investors which in addition to Omidyar
and Gray Matters Capital (see below) include Learn Capital (lead investor,
see below); Jasmine Social Investments, a New Zealand based family charity
investor; the D.o.b Foundation, a Dutch charity which 'invests in and
supports social entrepreneurs who identify commercial opportunities in
social issues' (company website), and which is a partner of the Acumen
Fund; the Hilti Foundation, another family foundation based in Liechtenstein that 'supports worldwide social, cultural and educational projects that
make a sustainable contribution to social development'; and LGT Venture
Philanthropy, funded by the Liechtenstein royal family.

According to its major funders, Bridge International's 'innovative
for-profit model has been designed and successfully tested to provide a

sustainable, scalable approach to education'. BIA's franchising technique provides a complete 'school in a box' which local managers can operate at an extremely low cost, but on a profitable basis. These profits, in turn, are supposed to help fund the development of additional schools in the network. Building on its Kenya schools, Bridge International plans to expand into additional countries in sub-Saharan Africa, establishing 1,800 schools by 2015. Once at capacity, it is claimed that these schools will also create jobs and provide income for 15,000 education workers in local communities.

> Bridge International extends access to primary education in Africa, demonstrating the power of for-profit innovation to transform lives.
> (http://www.omidyar.com/portfolio/bridge-international-academies)

The language deployed in the BIA materials and the many commentaries have elements of both 'silver bullet' and 'great challenge' claims, in as much as the 'project aims to develop scalable systems that will use new capital to strengthen local expertise to extend the reach of low-cost private schools to poor children in India and Kenya'. The programme also involves teacher training and leadership capacity building as part of the 'school in a box'. This includes a School Manager Manual which provides a detailed step-by-step set of processes that cover all financial, operational, instructional and human-resource management issues. This approach is compared to that of other large-scale chains-of-service businesses, such as McDonalds (see E. G. West Centre EFA Working Paper No. 10 – the Centre, directed by James Tooley, sees Bridge as a model of good practice in developing low-cost private schools). The company is also developing its own impact and evaluation systems. The model includes:

- the time from conception to door-opening for all schools is five months
- school buildings are constructed for less than $2,000 per classroom
- parents are charged 295 Kenyan Shillings ($4) per month, which is estimated to be less than the unofficial fees charged at local free government schools
- each school will be expected to enrol up to 1,000 children and to become profitable within one year of opening
- both school managers and teachers are employed from the local community and while their base salaries are low they receive bonuses for increasing enrolments and the on-time payment of school fees
- lesson plans are developed at the head office and a particular emphasis is placed on ensuring that children have a good understanding of English.

('Kenya: A Commercial Approach to Slum Education',
Ratio Magazine, 4 May 2010)

Parents pay fees and school owners pay bills using an electronic M-PESA mobile phone system – no money changes hands at school level.

The *Nextbillion* website notes that 'electronic payment mechanisms, provided they are convenient, cheap and secure enough, can propel new business models which in turn can make serious inroads in the delivery of products and services at the base of the pyramid'. Mobile phones are also being used to pay school fees in Uganda, where the mobile phone company Zain launched its Zap school fees service in May 2010. To help promote its launch Zain awarded 300 students free schooling and distributed sh50 million in educational grants to the 20 schools with the highest number of school fees transactions ('Zap targets school fees', *Allafrica.com*, 23 May 2010).

According to Steve Hardgrave, Managing Director at Gray Ghost Ventures, another BIA funder, the 'aim will be to build upon the success of the use of microfinance in other sectors of the economy to help dramatically expand access to quality education for poor children in the developing world, and this will have a game-changing effect on poverty alleviation' (Deutsche Bank Press Release, 'Deutsche Bank Americas Foundation to finance private schools in Kenya and India', 24 September 2008). By July 2010 twelve schools had already been opened in the slums of Nairobi and the company announced its plan to rapidly scale up. In order to support the expansion of its school network, the number of full-time employees increased from 8 to 58 during 2009, with 36 based in schools and 22 based at headquarters working on land acquisition, construction, instruction & curriculum and research & marketing. By May 2010 the company employed 88 people, 66 in schools.

By March 2011 there were 200 employees and about 3,000 students. And the company website said, 'the company is aggressively hiring in all departments – everything from instruction to operations to software development'. At the end of 2009 the company announced the following:

> When we launched Bridge International Academies, most people thought it would be impossible to run high quality schools on a profitable basis while charging less than $4 per month. Bridge International's first school that launched last January ended its first 12 months of operations virtually breakeven (showing a loss of $400).

Pierre Omidyar says that 'Bridge International provides a compelling example of high-impact entrepreneurship, which is not only extending access to education, but also serving as a model of how others can ignite social change through for-profit innovation'. Bridge also runs a Fellowship programme which takes self-funding fellows to Africa to take part in its teacher training and organisational development programmes, and the development of 'instructional products'. The BIA is a radical alternative to traditional forms of development aid, bringing new actors, energies and sensibilities to bear upon the problem of access to education.

Following the money

A key element of social enterprise and social capitalism is of course, as outlined above, money. People with 'good ideas' need to find backers who believe that their ideas will 'work', have an 'impact' and generate 'returns' as social outcomes or as profit. In this case it is interesting to follow some of the money trails through the investors in Bridge International. As indicated above, they are a mix of foundations, venture philanthropists, and commercial capital investors (see Figure 4.1). Again the network as presented here is of necessity selective and indicative rather than exhaustive.

At the hub of the network is Learn Capital, formerly Revolution Learning, a lead investor in BIA. It is a US-based venture capital firm which concentrates exclusively on the global education sector.

> We invest in innovative learning content, platforms, and services. Our companies are engaged in the transformation of educational engagement, access, and effectiveness in formalized schooling and consumer settings throughout the world.
>
> (Learn Capital website)

Learn has 'Invested in thousands of innovative new schools. Devised the key data-driven decision platform for [school] districts. Launched a major facilities funding vehicle for top schools. Introduced 3D stealth learning to mainstream audiences' (Learn Capital website). More specifically, Learn's investments include Edmodo (a social learning network for K12 students), Lafafa (an English language learning and school system based in China), and OpenEd Solutions (a 'blended' on/off-line learning service to support schools and districts). Learn's managing partner is Tom Vander Ark, former executive director of the BMGF and former US school superintendent in Washington state. He is also a partner in Vander Ark/Ratcliff, a strategic consulting firm which works with profit/not-for-profit and government organisations and has a particular focus on education. Katherine Vander Ark, a company manager at VanderArk/Ratcliff, worked for a year with Gray Matters Capital, in Hyderabad 'to strengthen low-cost private schools' (Learn Capital website). Tom Vander Ark also blogs for Edreformer.com, advises the National Association of Charter Schools Authorizers, and sits on the boards of MLA Partner Schools and Strive for College. In 2009 he wrote a working paper for the American Enterprise Institute for Public Policy Research (a corporately funded think tank and lobby organisation), 'Private Capital and Public Education: Toward Quality at Scale', in which he says: 'The dramatic increase in young software billionaires has been accompanied by a dramatic increase in education philanthropy that is oriented more towards new ventures and is less bounded by the roles and rules of traditional charity' (Vander Ark, 2009, p. 21) and goes on

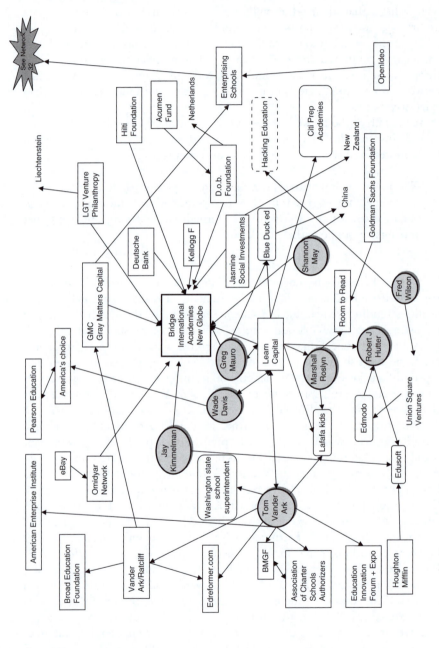

Figure 4.1 Learn Capital.

to argue that: 'Private investment in for-profit enterprises will be critical to expanding global access to quality education … ' (p. 25).

Learn partner Robert J. Hutter was co-founder with Jay Kimmelman of Edusoft and is responsible for Learn's Edmodo investment; Edmodo is also invested in by Union Square Ventures, a company headed by Fred Wilson, also an education reform blogger, and organiser with Learn Capital of the conference Hacking Education at which he argued that 'the public education system of this country is badly broken … And, of course, I believe that the Internet is a tool that we can use … to reinvent the way we educate ourselves'. Among the 'edupreneurial' solutions mentioned at the conference were Edmodo and MangaHigh (another Learn investment) and the work of Enterprising Schools (Gray Matters Capital) in India. Finally, Learn partner Wade Davis was previously involved with the development of America's Choice, a school improvement company bought by Pearson in 2010 (see Chapters 5 and 6).

This example from the social, political and financial network in which BIA is set gives some indication of the joining-up of method, money, ideology and discourse in relation to social enterprise and so-called corporate social capitalism.[3] There are links, overlaps and interrelations between sectors and types of organisations and between related initiatives and 'investments'. In the network, commercial online educational products and services are related to low-cost schools for the poor in Africa and India, to the US Charter school movement, and criticisms of US public education, to NGOs and advocacy organisations, to social investors, and venture philanthropists. There is an interest in educational opportunities in China, in personalized, online, social learning, and in school improvement 'solutions' – there are a variety of 'grand challenges' and related 'silver bullets'. The network is epistemically integrated through a shared language of 'products' and services, like pedagogical software and other 'instructional products', and a mutually reinforcing commitment to enterprise or market-based 'solutions' to educational problems. There is a collective focus on methods like PPPs, training and capacity building, fellowships and school-improvement techniques. There is here a shadow (Wolch, 1990) infrastructure of educational provision and services and Western models of practice, organisation and pedagogy are being developed, donated and sold (see Chapter 5) and scaled-up at 'home' and 'abroad'. Reform, social enterprise, equity and opportunity also work to create new business possibilities and open up new markets. There is also a subtext of 'roll-back' and 'roll-out' neo-liberalism here, critiques of the 'failing' state and celebration of market-based alternatives. The market is constantly spawning new sites of such discourse articulation – meetings, blogs, conferences and so on. This again can be understood as neo-liberal work, both in a political and in a practical financial sense. Critiques and advocacy are set in relation to funded alternatives and indicators of 'success'. This is a diverse but arguably a dense and well-integrated network; there are certainly a good number of recurrences and overlaps. It is related to and overlaps with a further network (Figure 4.2) which is presented later.

Opportunity and affordability

The second example of activity, stemming from the brokerage work of the CGI, and the third related example of 'market solutions' to education problems, are briefer. The second concerns a US-based non-profit microfinance organisation, Opportunity International (see also Chapter 3). Opportunity International operates in 28 countries through 43 microfinance institutions. It raises funds from charitable contributions, government grants and debt and equity from third parties. Opportunity International

> ... announced at the Clinton Global Initiative's Fifth Annual Meeting that it will expand its Banking on Education program to five additional countries over the next 24 months. Opportunity will commit USD 10 million to its education finance program, which provides loans for entrepreneurs to open schools in poor areas where it is difficult for children, particularly girls, to access public schools ... Opportunity currently invests in over 200 private schools in five countries, with loans ranging from USD 500 to USD 25,000 for terms of two to five years. The program reached over 8,000 children in 2007 ... Opportunity aims to improve educational opportunities for up to 250,000 children by 2012.
>
> In addition to providing loans to entrepreneurs to start and expand schools, Opportunity offers interest-bearing tuition savings accounts and school fee loans for parents who cannot afford their children's education.
>
> > (http://www.microcapital.org/microcapitalorg-story-opportunity-
> > international-expands-education-finance-program-with-10m-
> > for-entrepreneurs-to-open-schools-in-poor-neighborhoods)

Opportunity grounds and legitimates its decision to expand its Banking on Education programme with specific reference to James Tooley's research.

> In a *five-year study* comparing 'schools for the poor' in India, China, Nigeria, Kenya and Ghana with government schools, Dr. James Tooley, Professor of Education Policy at Newcastle University, observed that schools for the poor were superior to government schools. Not only are they more cost efficient, they 'offer flexible payment options, leading to reduced drop out rates in tough financial times. Most microschools are located in close proximity to poor households. This makes parents feel secure about sending their daughters to schools and also helps them save on transportation costs'.

In both this example and the next, we see James Tooley once again as a key policy entrepreneur and *animateur*, or what the Affordable Private Schools Symposium (APSS) calls a 'thought leader'. APSS is organised by the Gray Matters Capital Foundation (GMC), an off-shoot of Gray Matters Ventures, which describes itself as 'a private operating foundation that researches and co-creates initiatives with local partners to build sustainable and replicable business models for the benefit of underserved populations' (APSS website). Like Opportunity International, GMC is a microfinance organisation, which works alongside 'sister enterprises', the Gray Ghost Microfinance Fund and the Rockdale Foundation. As noted earlier, GMC is an investor in Bridge International. GMC was founded by Bob Pattillo, described on the GMC website as 'An entrepreneur and philanthropist'. It goes on to say, 'Prior to this career, Bob built and managed the 8th largest industrial real estate development firm in the United States. Along with his own social enterprises Bob sits on the board of directors of several microfinance organizations and investment funds' (www.graymatterscap. com, accessed 8 October 2010).

Gray Matters describes itself as an 'emerging brand of social investment' which 'excels at providing risk capital that is quick, flexible, and customized to the circumstances of the entrepreneur and the social venture. GMC deploys its $15 million fund into seed and early stage equity investments ranging from $250,000 to $2.0 million'. Education is only one of its fields of investment. Gray Matters works with the enterprises in which it invests, 'providing value-added governance', and seeks to develop indicators for its investments which work as a 'business tool' and as social-impact measures.

> GMC offers a unique blend of access to other social ventures and entre-preneurs, like-minded allies and co-investors, commitment from skilled developers, and an opportunity to be mentored by people of experience and character.
>
> (http://www.graymatterscap.com/investments)

One of GMC's 'ventures' is EnterprisingSchools.com, which appears to be based in India, and which in turn runs the Affordable Private Schools Symposium, at which in 2010, in Hyderabad, James Tooley and Jay Kimmelman were keynote speakers (see http://www.enterprisingschools. com, accessed 8 October 2010). APSS is a fascinating and telling example of the new, complex, and multifaceted relationships being established in the new education policy arenas.

At the 2009 symposium there were 40 organisations plus James Tooley (as the only individual) listed as participants (see Figure 4.2). Among these India is strongly represented but also Africa, China and Latin America. Participants included philanthropies (e.g. USAID,[4] Michael and Susan Dell Foundation), businesses (e.g. SONG Investment advisers, Indian School

Finance Company – see Chapter 3), Educomp Solutions Ltd (now part owned by Pearson, see Chapter 6), CfBT, Faulu Kenya Ltd, Sunshine Fortune Education Investment & Consultancy Co. Ltd (a Chinese company founded by James Tooley), microfinance banks (SKS, K-Rep Bank Ltd – see Chapter 3), as well as the Ghana Ministry of Education and Kenya Independent Schools Association.

Like the CGI and in relation to it, the APSS is a setting for advocacy and making relationships and doing deals, for putting funders, sponsors and donors in contact with businesses and innovators and national governments to create new education programmes and initiatives. These projects, programmes and initiatives then bring together philanthropies, charity and commercial banks, private equity, commercial providers, social enterprises and governments, and are producing a new generation of multinational education businesses, social enterprises and charities, some with diverse involvements in educational services and products.

> We're in Hyderabad this week, reporting from the inaugural Affordable Private School Symposium, organized by Gray Matters Capital. After a long day being steeped in conversations about this new space, the overwhelming thought is the time is now! There is a sense of being in the right place at the right time. A sensation of being part of a sector that is moving forward.
>
> Let me back up. Affordable Private Schools are social enterprises, providing a reliable source of education for children living in low-income urban areas. Families are considered clients, with the right to demand a quality education. School owners put an emphasis on quality and efficiency, justifying the modest tuition charged that allows them to cover their expenses.
>
> (http://beyondprofit.com/index.php?s=tooley,
> accessed 25 August 2010)

In all of this the distinctions between businesses, social enterprises, not-for-profits and philanthropies is blurred. Relationships – initiatives, investments, partnerships, ownership, programmes, advocacy – are multifaceted, and people move between and speak on behalf of these different organisations in different roles (see and view together Figures 3.1, 4.1 and 4.2). The Affordable Private Schools Symposium, as a micro-assemblage and networking event, is an example of the new, complex, and multifaceted relationships being established in new sites of policy.

At the risk of trying the reader's patience and energy, I offer one final example of policy networks, networking and policy advocacy, in this case a virtual network, but again overlapping and interrelated with the previous one – to some extent the medium here is part of the message.

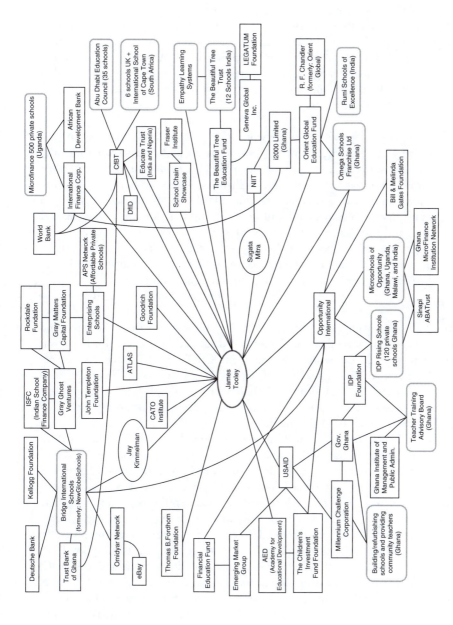

Figure 4.2 James Tooley travels to the remotest regions on Earth.

Enterprising schools[5]

This is a ready-made network, a virtual 'globalising microspace', organised by Gray Matters Capital, but many of the participants also meet at the annual APSS (as above). This is another opportunity for networking and persuasion, for telling stories and presenting powerpoints, performing 'impact' for funders and other audiences, rehearsing silver bullets, accumulating knowledge, social capital and building trust. A look at the members and their missions, languages and relationships provides some further sense of the discursive and ideological 'connective issue' which holds these organisations together.

> Enterprising Schools is a network that encourages collaboration and knowledge exchange among practitioners and individuals globally working towards transforming the affordable private sector. The online portal serves as the only comprehensive online resource – offering commentary and discussions on the affordable private school sector, a repository of research and publications, updates on the latest market data, and profiles of global sector players.
>   Enterprising Schools challenges each stakeholder to collaboratively work to shape and advance the sector so that we can transform the lives of students across the globe with greater scale and impact.
>
> (http://184.73.202.230/about-us)

Among the participants listed in 2010, and organisations do join and leave, there were several we have met and discussed before. Again, India was well represented. Organisations included: CfBT again, which has offices in Chennai and Hyderabad (see Chapter 3) and which is involved in a range of activities including a Whole School Improvement Programme (WSIP), preschool education and managing nurseries, teacher supply and development, and English medium teaching. Educomp, again, a large and very diverse Indian 'education services provider' with 27 offices worldwide including India (20), Canada, USA, Sri Lanka and Singapore – Educomp is a partner of the Raffles Education Corporation (see Chapter 6). Gyan Shala is an Indian social enterprise which seeks to offer 'low cost but assured high quality basic education' to 'poor and urban slum children' in Ahmedadabad, where in 2007 it began by running 300 primary classes. It has developed a computer-aided learning package and is interested in PPPs and hopes to run contracted-out state schools. It is supported by, among others, Tata, the World Bank, the Dell Foundation and the ICICI Bank. iDiscoveri Consulting is an Indian social enterprise which focuses on 'leadership and talent in workplaces' and seeks to 'renew education in India' with its 'cutting edge curriculum and teaching methods'. It aims to partner with schools and has worked with ICICI, Wipro and Deutsche Bank. The IDEX Fellowship in Social Enterprise is run by Oglethorpe

University in the US with Gray Matters Capital and sends Fellows to get involved with Affordable Private Schools in Hyderabad and work closely with a school leader 'through careful observation and dialogue'. The first ten Fellows were recruited in 2010. GMC has set up 'a schooling rating system' to compare and 'benchmark school standards' and if standards are met schools are eligible to take part in a school voucher programme run by GMC. IDEX has a 'theory of change' that 'young adults are the next generation of leaders for solving world issues' and aims to produce 'teachers committed to addressing structural inequalities'. The Director, Sreeratna Kancherla, previously directed Social-Impact International (India) co-founded by UK philanthropist Peter Wheeler (see Ball & Junemann, 2012). Intellecap, a microfinance company based in Mumbai, has connections to the World Bank (see Chapter 3). The Lead Now Foundation, based in Nigeria, is based on South Africa's Teach for South Africa programme, funded by Deloitte-Touche, which in turn is based on Teach for America and England's Teach First programmes (See Ball & Junemann, 2012). The aim is to create a corps of teacher-leaders. Micro-Credit Ratings International Ltd – which does what the name suggests, has Basix Bank as a client.

Omega Schools Franchise Ltd 'is partnering with school proprietors to create a sustainable large chain of branded low-cost private schools in Ghana. They are bringing private sector investment to the hundreds of low-cost private schools ...' (Omega website). James Tooley is currently the chairman of Omega Schools Franchise Ltd and a Trustee of Omega Schools Foundation. He is also the Education Advisor, directing the development of the Omega curriculum. The co-founder and Chief Executive is Ken Donkoh, who previously worked for Oxfam and USAID: 'Its embryonic chain of five (5) schools located in peri-urban areas fringing Accra were filled to their capacities on the week of opening. The sixth and seventh schools are set to open in the first week of January 2011' (Omega website). The start-up cost is $60,000 for each school and they function on a standard model which has elements in common with Bridge International.

- An innovative all-inclusive no hidden cost daily fee payment system, ensures that we rope in a lot more lower-income families who otherwise may not be able to afford bulk term fees.
- Built in the daily fee is a micro insurance policy which ensures that every child in our schools can complete their schooling even in the event of death or permanent disability of the breadwinner of their family.
- A fifteen (15) free school days per year ensures that children are able to attend school on all days including times when their parents may not be able to pay the daily fee.
- Our daily fee includes a nutritious hot lunch each day and scheduled mass deworming programmes, ensuring good health and nutrition for all our children.

Open Ideo.com is an online platform for 'creative thinkers' which has taken on the 'challenge' sponsored by Enterprising Schools of 'increasing the access to low-cost and appropriate learning tools for affordable private schools'. The Pratham Education Foundation, based in India, is a large NGO which has won the Indian Business Leaders Award in the Social Enterprise category. It focuses on the educational needs of 'underprivileged children in India', it runs Read India, a literacy programme, does 'focused interventions' in schools, teacher training, and publishes the Annual Status of Education Report. On its Board of Trustees are representatives of ICICI, KKR (see Chaper 6), McKinsey and Suney Varkey, founder of GEMS (see Ball, 2007). Funders include HSBC, ICICI, Deutsche Bank and the World Bank. Rumi Education, based in Hyderabad and founded by James Tooley and Richard Chandler, as noted in the previous chapter, runs a chain of private schools. Teach for India and Teach to Lead are further iterations of Teach for America (another silver bullet), heavily backed, as in England, by McKinsey – three representatives sit on its Board. It is also supported by Tata, ICICI and Goldman Sachs and has links to the Ashoka Foundation. It focuses its teachers in 'low income and private schools' and aims to generate an influential alumni group. It aims to foster talent and achieve 'measurable impact'. The Mitchell Group is a US consulting firm that runs a large number (74+) of USAID projects. It works in India and Africa and elsewhere, in partnerships, to achieve 'sustainable development' and offers 'practical solutions', monitoring and evaluation tools, and has some involvement in basic education and teacher training. The Teacher Foundation is a not-for-profit based in Bangalore, supported by the Shraddha Trust. It works to develop schools and educators and leadership capabilities through its proprietary tool 'school improvement framework', early years curriculum development and research and evaluation in partnership with schools. Among its funders are Tata and the GE Foundation. SKS Education Society, a foundation of SKS Bank (see Chapter 3) runs 16 Bodhi Academies, private schools in four districts in Andhra Pradesh launched in 2009, which charge INR 160–220 ($3–5) a month for English-medium education based on the 'play way method'. Dignitas is a US-based not-for-profit working in Nairobi to run a 'leadership institute' to 'empower indigenous leaders'. Vita Beans: Neural Solutions is an education technology company based in Bangalore which works in partnerships with schools, offering 'solutions for schools' based on 'learning, assessment and interaction' using online games, tests and kits and runs a 'start-up' called Vita Beans Apps that 'help you learn and share knowledge using innovative ways that are more fun, more effective and more intelligent!' Finally, Escuela Nueva is a non-profit organisation based in Colombia, but now also working with the Vietnam Ministry of Education and in 16 other countries, which focuses on the 'school as a basis of change' and works towards 'quality, efficiency and sustainability' in schooling. Its founder Vicky Colbert won the 2011 Henry R Krais Prize for social entrepreneurship (part funded by Tata and the World Bank); she also received Bill Clinton's Global Citizen Award and her work has also been commended by the Ashoka, Skoll and Schwab Foundations, all social enterprise funders. In 2009 she addressed the World Innovation Summit on Education. Escuela Nueva appears in the School Chain Showcase, which is run by the Fraser Institute (see Chapter 2), of which Tooley is a consultant.

Many of the themes noted in the previous discussion recur here but also Enterprising Schools, in a package and an infrastructure, is again a shadow alternative to state provision in almost all aspects of education – funding, training, CPD, recruitment, school management and leadership, school improvement, accreditation, curriculum and assessment. Social enterprise is the fundamental method for change but again there is a mix of and interplay between for-profit companies, not-for-profit social enterprises, venture capital and venture philanthropy. Solutions may be 'given' or may be sold. This is a dual process that Shamir (2008) calls 'enfolding', within which the 'economization of the state and civil society' is mirrored by 'the moralization of the market' (Shamir, 2008, p. 2). It is also a transfer and exchange system; it brings Fellows to work and learn, it 'borrows' policy ideas from the West. It brings innovations and 'cutting-edge' techniques to bear upon problems of social disadvantage and engages with marginalised groups. There are a lot of claims made for originality, creativity and innovation. There is a reiteration of the language of poverty, disadvantage, inequality, alongside quality, efficiency and impact, and partnerships – involving low-cost private, contracted out and state schools. The role of IT is significant again – apps, learning packages, online environments and assessment tools are on offer. The organisations are developing brands, proprietary tools and methods, as instructional tools, curriculum materials and pedagogies. There is again the significance of microfinance of various forms – commercial banks and charitable investing. The USA is very well represented and certain target locations reappear – Andhra Pradesh (Hyderabad), Kenya and Nigeria in particular. The Tata Foundation is a donor to almost all of the Indian social enterprises and foundations, the World Bank is much in evidence, as is ICICI Bank and SKS and Basix, and USAID recurs. Some of the leading global social enterprise funders and supporters are also involved, in particular Ashoka and Skoll.

Social capitalism and neo-liberalism and hybridities

In a variety of ways the USA is a key player in these new forms of philanthropy and new opportunities for business, both 'at home' and abroad. Desmond Bermingham of the Center for Global Development recently argued that: 'There is a tremendous opportunity for the United States to demonstrate global political leadership in the international movement to provide a decent education for all children and all young people' (2009, p. 1) and advocated the creating of a 'Global fund for Education'.

Put succinctly, entrenched problems of educational development and educational quality and access are now being addressed by the involvement of
social enterprises and edu-businesses in the delivery of educational services,
both privately and on behalf of the state. The latter is evident in the US
within the No Child Left Behind programme (Burch, 2009), and in England in the Academies programme (Ball, 2007). The former are increasingly
evident in the setting-up of private storefront schools by local entrepreneurs
and the creation of school chains by multinational education companies in
relation to the attempts of developing societies to achieve their Millennium
Development Goals and to provide mass access to basic education. More and
more, international aid and philanthropy are no longer 'donated' as grants
to governments and NGOs but rather are 'invested' in edu-businesses and in
the development of market and social-enterprise solutions to educational
problems. Business methods and social-enterprise initiatives are seen as more
effective ways of achieving wider access to and improved quality of education than, it is argued, can be achieved by governments or via traditional
aid or charity. This approach is sometimes referred to as *Corporate Social
Capitalism* – based on 'investments that address social challenges and result
in sustainable business' (Tony Friscia, AMR Research inc., 2009). The shifts
and moves involved here are made up of and driven by a complex set of
political and economic processes involving advocacy, by policy entrepreneurs
like James Tooley and transnational advocacy networks like the Atlas
Foundation Liberty Network, business interests (new profit opportunities),
'new' philanthropy, and changes in the form and modalities of the state.
Each of these elements needs to be attended to in the analysis of the new
global education policy paradigm.

The CGI and the other networks and assemblages sketched in here aim
their activities primarily at low-income countries, and the low-cost, private
school initiatives indicated above are targeted at these countries and indeed
are concentrated in particular countries which are 'receptive', in one way or
another, and which offer opportunities for profit – like Nigeria, Ghana,
Kenya and India. The private schools created are represented as supple-
menting existing state provision to achieve national and international policy
goals. As Ong (2007, p. 6) suggests: 'Neoliberal calculations identify opti-
mizing spaces and populations in relation to global market opportunities'.
In 2007, School Ventures and the Economist Intelligence Unit launched
the African Schools Investment Index (ASPI) as an 'analytical tool for
investors, policy makers, philanthropists and educationalists' and it compares
'the attractiveness of African markets as destination for private investment'.
Nonetheless, these initiatives are epistemically and literally joined up to
critiques of public schooling and pressures for change and reform moves
(charter schooling, contracting out) in Western countries, as in the examples
in the networks outlined above.

What I am trying to capture and convey here, in this rather superficial
review of some of the forms of 'enterprise' and the enterprising people in

new global social and education policy, is the increasingly complex and opaque crossings, blurrings, interweavings, or hybridities, that constitute and animate this neo-liberal landscape of enterprise. People, money and ideas move through these networks and organisations and across the boundaries which they span. The organisations involved display a variety of different and changing mixes of charitable, social enterprising and business identities and commitments. Financially and organisationally and morally their status and standing is often, at face value, unclear. We can also see new complex careers in all of this as actors move between the state, the third and forth sectors and business, take up different moral positions and mix these in composite job portfolios. They are employees, consultants, trustees, entrepreneurs, philanthropists, advocates and *animateurs*, engaged in a variety of opportunities/interests/commitments, which are difficult sometimes to pin down and unpack. Where the social ends and enterprise begins, and what not-for-profit means, is sometimes difficult to discern at organisational and individual levels. As Clarke and Newman put it:

> Established typologies (the distinction between state and market or the hierarchy, markets and networks framework) fall short of new organisational forms and governance arrangements that are identified through such terms as boundary blurring or hybridity. Such terms mark the problem of naming these new arrangements, but bring problems of their own.
>
> (http://www.espanet-italia.net/conference2009/call-for-abstracts/
> 18.php, accessed 21 May 2010)

I might be legitimately criticised for putting too many disparate processes and varieties of actors within this assemblage of transformational impetuses but I hope to have shown, prima facie at least, that this heterogeneous field of activity is 'joined-up' in various ways in networked social relations and through an interrelated and cognate language of concepts and practices. These are 'unruly historical geographies of an evolving, interconnected project' (Brenner, Peck & Theodore, 2010, p. 8). That is, they make up a discursive formation – a certain regularity or unity between statements, objects, concepts, within the broad field within which knowledge is produced and embedded in a rule-governed set of material practices. The engine of knowledge here is clearly not the individual actors but the discursive community – and that discourse and its subjects and practices we might call neo-liberalism. The opacity of all this can be mitigated somewhat if we think about which speakers are privileged and 'get heard' within the transformation of the public sector (Shamir, 2008, p. 68), their 'interests' and how the sites and domains of the discourse effect the objects produced – essentially a dual process of commodification and financialisation, and moral entrepreneurship (Shamir, 2008, p. 2).

What is exemplified here is 'enterprise' writ small (microfinance and low-cost schools franchises) and large (a global social enterprise infrastructure, see Figure 4.3). As Rose puts it: 'The idea of enterprise links up a seductive ethics of the self, a powerful critique of contemporary institutional and political reality, and an apparently coherent design for the radical transformation of contemporary social arrangements' (Rose, 2007, p. 19). This is, in other words, the neo-liberal imaginary at work, a reworking of the objects and subjects of education and social policy.

What I have been trying to represent and explore here, to borrow from Ong (2006, p. 499), are 'new spaces of entangled possibilities' which are constituted and enacted within new global education policy networks. That is, new spaces of neo-liberalism and of the 'economization of the social'. I do not want to overwrite the extent of or influence of the developments and initiatives described here, although they are scaling up fast, particularly in India, but there are clearly aspects here of what Peck and Tickell (2002) call the 'normalization of neo-liberal logics' (p. 24), but often in 'impure' forms and as messy hybridities and in diverse partnerships. These are processes which both act 'on' and act 'against' the state and state-sector education in a variety of ways and through a variety of relationships. However, Peck and Tickell also argue that we must be circumspect about holding neo-liberalism as responsible for or evident in everything and they go on to emphasise the need for a qualitative understanding of neo-liberalism 'in all of its spatially variegated, institutionally-specific and historically changing forms' (p. 21). 'New' philanthropy, social capitalism and social enterprise may well be examples of these changing forms. The policy mobilities which are evident here are complex. On the one hand, as Blaut (1993) suggests, 'diffusionism involves a belief that inventiveness is scarce and concentrated in a few advanced and progressive places' (pp. 46–47), a kind of 'spatial elitism' (1993, p. 12) or neo-colonialism. On the other, it might be argued that the 'enrolment' of local entrepreneurs and advocates weighs against this, and it is certainly possible to see distinct vernacular inflections in many of the new social enterprises addressing educational issues, especially those in India.

Notes

1 In some ways the 'old/new' philanthropy distinction is rhetorical as much as substantive but it does indicate some different emphases in terms of tracing the relationships between giving and effects and wanting to participate in the planning for those effects (see http://www.tacticalphilanthropy.com/2007/05/old-vs-new-philanthropy, accessed 12 June 2011).

2 Bronfman is former co-chairman of the Seagram Company and the founder of the Andrea and Charles Bronfman Philanthropies.

3 See Tony Friscia, 'The 2009 Clinton Global Initiative: Corporate Social Capitalism Is the New Basis of Global Competition', 2 October 2009

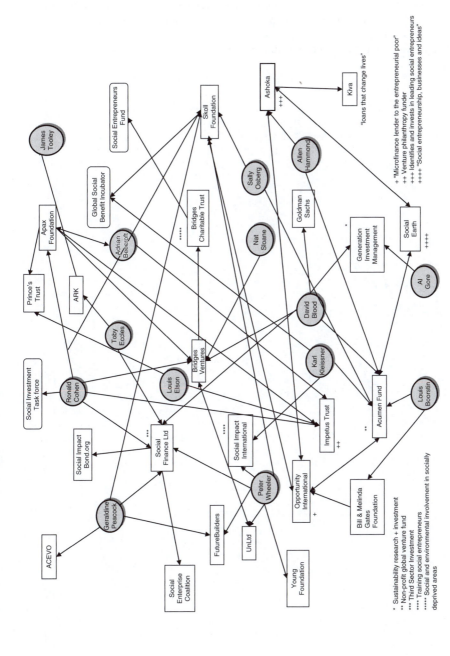

+ "Microfinance lender to the entrepreneurial poor"
++ Venture philanthropy funder
+++ Identifies and invests in leading social entrepreneurs
++++ "Social entrepreneurship, businesses and ideas"

"loans that change lives"

* Sustainability research + investment
** Non-profit global venture fund
*** Third Sector Investment
**** Training social entrepreneurs
***** Social and environmental involvement in socially deprived areas

Figure 4.3 Global enterprise philanthropy.

(http://www.amrresearch.com/content/view.aspx?compURI=tcm:7–48415, accessed 25 August 2010).

4 USAID is described as an independent federal government agency that receives overall foreign policy guidance from the Secretary of State. It works with more than 3,500 American companies and more than 300 US-based voluntary organisations.

5 I am very grateful to Diego Santori for his help with this section.

5 Policy as profit

Selling and exporting policy

In this chapter and the next I will address some different but related aspects of global education policy, aspects which are almost totally ignored in the current literatures on policy transfer and policy mobilities. That is, the role of policy itself as a profit opportunity for global edu-businesses – both the 'selling' and picking up the theme of philanthropy from the previous chapter, the *giving away* of policy and education services, and the participation of these businesses in national and international education policy communities and in the work of policy mobility. As Holden argues: 'The literature on policy transfer has paid insufficient attention to the role of commercial interests in the transfer of policy' (Holden, 2009, p. 331). As in previous chapters, I will focus on some specific examples of the business activities of multinational education businesses (MNEBs)[1] and business philanthropies in relation to policy, as part of what Larner (2002) calls 'a new specialist elite'. Again the point is to attend to how *'actually existing'* neo-liberalism gets done – or what Brenner and Theodore (2002, p. 351) refer to as 'the contextual *embeddedness* of neo-liberal restructuring projects'. Thus, I will explore the changing relationships between business, education policy and nation states, and again the increasingly important role of business and corporate philanthropy in 'solving' education policy problems, and again touch upon the concomitant changes in the form and modalities of the contemporary state. These developments reinforce the point made previously, that education policy analysis can no longer sensibly be limited to within the nation state – the fallacy of methodological territorialism – and extend this to argue that policy analysis must also extend its purview beyond the state and the role of multilateral agencies and NGOs to include transnational business practices.

The privatisation(s) referred to here are complex, multifaceted and inter-related. They can be understood in relation to the development of a set of complex relationships between: (i) organisational changes in public sector institutions (recalibration and 'improvement'); (ii) new state forms and modalities (governance, networks and performance management); (iii) the privatisation of the state itself; and (iv) the interests of 'restless' capital and processes of commodification (public services as a profit opportunity and the provision of 'effective' public service provision). I shall try to indicate how each of these processes is embedded in the other and will return to a consideration of their interrelationships in the concluding discussion.

What is being argued here is that the participation of businesses within policy is a key mechanism, and a beneficiary, of education reform and the reform of the state, but not always an end in itself; rather, it is part of a 'judicious mix' of political strategies and a changing balance of relations among different kinds of institutions, apparatuses and agencies (Jessop, 2002, p. 50). On the one hand, there may well appear to be a logical inevitability to the processes of privatisation(s) in current political circumstances, a 'seemingly irresistible pressure' (Larbi, 1999, p. 5) towards the 'obvious', the *doxa*, of privatisation as a solution to state problems, as I shall indicate later. On the other hand, not all experiments in privatisation are successful or sustainable. Nonetheless, it is important to attend to the increasing variety of 'business opportunities', including new forms of outsourcing, contracting and public–private partnership, which are emerging as more of the business of the education state is divested and 'privatised' or 'shared' with business. The trends in each form of privatisation are different and need to be considered separately and together.[2] I will proceed by examining more or less briefly three interrelated layers of policy and their privatisations. The plural here is important in signalling the variety of forms of privatisation involved. I shall also try to indicate the same mix of ideological and material neo-liberalism in each layer. They are:

> Organisational recalibration, 'selling' improvement and mediating policy
> The colonisation of the infrastructures of policy
> Exporting and 'selling' policy: a global market in policy ideas

Organisational recalibration, 'selling' improvement and mediating policy

One of the forms of the privatisation of education which has received very little attention, despite the fact that increasingly education businesses are an integral part of the education policy process as policy is enacted within the workaday world of schools, colleges and universities, is the retailing of policy solutions and 'improvement' to schools. Here the 'cultural circuit' of capitalism (Thrift, 2005, p. 118) touches very directly upon the daily activities of schooling and its social relationships.

> Policy researchers ... need to pay more attention to the effects of educational privatization on local school governance. The research is either silent or offers superficial treatment of how educational privatization can open doors for outside vendors to exercise political

influence over the design and administration of local accountability reforms.

(Burch, 2006, p. 2605)

This sort of business activity, at school (and college and university) level, includes the selling of CPD (continuing professional development), consultancy, training, support and 'improvement' and management services, as well as a whole variety of technical, support and back-office services. That is, the selling of policy as a retail commodity. There is not the space here to convey a full sense of the variety of such services which are on offer, but I will give some examples from some current company brochures and websites (see Ball, 2007 for details).[3]

The processes of education reform and school improvement and the concomitant policy turbulence are all business opportunities for education service companies, especially so as state funded, national and local support agencies are subject to cutbacks. Reforms offer to these companies what Saltman (2007, p. 21) calls 'silver linings and golden opportunities' or more dramatically possibilities of 'capitalizing on disaster' (the title of his book). Increasingly these companies act as linkage devices, 'interpreters' of policy operating between the state and public sector organisations – making reform sensible and manageable. Thus, Cambridge Education, a UK-based MNEB (more of which later), asserts that its 'extensive range of INSET training and consultancy, CPD training courses and teaching resources offers schools a variety of professional development opportunities to further raise standards of teaching and learning in your school' (Cambridge Education website). These professional development 'opportunities', initially developed in the context of the pressures of education reform in England, are presented as generic and as 'research based' and can be applied to any school anywhere, although each provider also claims that their 'product' is unique. For example, Cambridge have been working to improve the public schools in St Petersburg, Florida, USA, by means of 'cultural change'.

> School this year is different for all the students in the Petersburg City Public Schools. The schools have a private educational partner, Cambridge Education, to help improve the schools. For 200 students in grades six through nine, there are 'smaller learning communities' in four core subject areas that help students focus and engage more. But Cambridge and school officials say the changes go beyond the 200 students – that there is a cultural change that is taking root in the school system where education is valued and students want to learn. 'It's a systemic approach to bring about systemic change,' Dr. Alvera Parrish, superintendent said of Cambridge's way of bringing about improvement in the schools. The difference is one that Trevor Yates, vice president with Cambridge Education, attributes to a

cultural change. Yates said that the Cambridge methodology is research-based and different from what most districts do.

Cambridge Education website

America's Choice, a US school improvement company, recently bought by Pearson Education (see Chapter 6), has a similar sales pitch. That is:

> A comprehensive, coherent, research-based solution for schools— elementary, K–8, middle, and high—that improves the performance of all students.
>
> For more than ten years, America's Choice has been a proven turn-around partner; we have helped over 1,000 schools across the country. We have the **results** you are looking for—improved student achievement, higher test scores, increased graduation rates, fewer discipline problems, and more effective leadership and teaching.

Such claims are impressive – offering across-the-board improvement in 'learning', achievement, discipline and leadership. Nord Anglia, a UK-based international education company, says:

> Our services in this area help schools, colleges and work-based learning providers to make improvements. Our focus is always on improving educational outcomes for learners. We have a strong track record of delivering effective and sustainable support worldwide. We have worked with the following clients:
>
> Learning and Skills Improvement Service in the UK
> The Department for Children, Schools and Families in the UK
> The National College in the UK
> The Bahrain Economic Development Board
> Qatar Supreme Education Council
> The Mawhiba Partnership in the Kingdom of Saudi Arabia
> The Abu Dhabi Education Council

These 'products' as 'solutions' to the problems of policy typically engage in what Fullan (2001) calls organisational 'reculturing', as in the case of Cambridge, and they normally draw their language and methods from business models of *change management*. What are being sold are the necessities of change, a new managerialist language and a new kind of self-belief and self-efficacy – as well as new organisational ecologies and identities.

> As LEA and school leaders you are faced with tremendous challenges. In a changing world full of new ideas and innovations, we can help you develop transformational learning organisations.

(Cocentra advert, *Times Educational Supplement*)

The language and especially the verbs these texts deploy conveys a sense of urgency and speed – they work 'swiftly and efficiently' and are 'focused', they deliver 'streamlining' and 'manageability'. They construct a new grammar and lexicon of organisational life and instil a particular kind of organisational reflexivity (Jessop, 2002).

> We work with schools who are not content to stand still ... provide schools with potent educational tools ... consultancy, professional development and coaching support.
>
> (Edison Schools UK brochure)

The power and meaning of the texts and the discourses of reform they carry play upon the fears and desires of the audience, which are 'called up' from policy and the pressures of reform. It is a saviour discourse that promises to deliver schools, leaders and teachers and students from failure, from the terrors of uncertainty and from the confusions of policy and from themselves – their own weaknesses. State policies, particularly those which employ school-based management and performance-management techniques, can thus create incentives and pressures for public sector providers to use private sector services. These techniques, which rest upon the granting of greater autonomy to institutions and which deploy processes of deconcentration within education systems, also produce standardised and normalised responses, in part through the work of the edu-businesses themselves. In relation to this, edu-businesses have a strong vested interest in deconcentration policies as providing a climate of necessity and in freeing up resources at the local level from which their services can be paid for. Based on research in the US, Burch (2006) makes a similar point; she looks in particular at the effects in this regard of No Child Left Behind policies in the US. She notes that vendors of services 'have sought to leverage NCLB mandates as part of their marketing strategies' (p. 2582) and goes on to identify some of the untoward effects of increased reliance on private providers:

> Some of the most significant developments in educational privatization are occurring out of the spotlight of the press and academics. Across the country, urban school systems are relying on the services and products of specialty-service providers to jump-start compliance with NCLB. These shifts may help some school districts to support more rapid and flexible exchange of data. However, these developments may also serve to detract reforming districts from their commitment to improving teaching for traditionally underserved students and to building collective capacity to sustain changes over time.
>
> (Burch, 2006, p. 2582)

She identifies four areas of business which are central to the new educational privatisations in relation to NCLB. They are: test development and preparation, data analysis and management, remedial services, and content area-specific programming. US school districts historically have contracted with outside vendors for services in each of these areas but NCLB has accelerated this trend considerably. As a result, she goes on to point out that 'changes in the field of educational privatization have increased firms' resource dependency on the Federal government'. According to one estimate (Jackson & Bassett, 2005), the 45 million tests currently done each year in the US as part of the NCLB programme are worth $517m to the private sector.

All of this, and measurement and 'improvement' in particular, draws on the 'disciplines' of business, management and social science and contributes to the production of new knowledge about schools and teachers – exams, tests, audits, appraisals, inspections, evaluations, reviews and performance management – and, in doing so, inserts and guarantees a 'regulated self-regulation'. The companies contribute to the infrastructure and effectivity of what Ozga (2008) calls 'governing knowledge', that is knowledge of a new kind – a regime of numbers – that constitutes a 'resource through which surveillance can be exercised' (p. 264). That is, the use of performance information of various kinds as 'a resource for comparison' (p. 267), addressed to improvements in quality and efficiency, by making nations, schools and students 'legible' (p. 268) – this is an infrastructure for performativity (see Chapter 2) – a point to which we shall return. This, as Brenner and Theodore (2002) remind us, is a process of creative destruction. The methods of organisational recalibration and improvement destabilise existing professionalisms and displace professional knowledges, and replace them with the organisational tropes of management, leadership and enterprise (Chapter 2), or more accurately the old and the new mix together to produce an unstable and contested hybrid terrain of 'projected spaces'.

The privatising of the public sector here, through the work of edu-businesses (like Tribal, America's Choice, The Place Group, Cambridge Education, Nord Anglia, A4e and so on – see Ball, 2007) is not done by taking services out of public sector control but rather through selling policy 'solutions' and via collaborations of various kinds with the public sector, although some are more meaningfully collaborative than others. Partnerships open up various kinds of flows between the sectors, flows of people, information and ideas, of language, methods, values and culture: 'states have a key role in promoting innovative capacities, technical competence and technology transfer ... often involving extensive collaboration' (Jessop, 2002, p. 121). Partnerships are a further aspect of the blurring between sectors as well as a profit opportunity to which I return later in this chapter.

The colonisation of the infrastructures of policy

This is the second layer of privatisations and is what Mahony, Menter and Hextall (2004) call 'the privatisation of policy'. What I am referring to here is the production by education and consultancy companies of policy 'texts' and policy ideas *for* and *within* the state, that is, the export of 'statework' to private providers and 'agencies', and the formation and dissemination of new policy discourses arising out of the participation of these companies in report writing, evaluations, advice, consultancy and recommendations. In other words, the representatives of the private sector operate inside of government and are part of the 'policy creation community' (Mahony, Menter et al., 2004). This increasingly occurs across all levels and forms of policy.

This involves a new generation of *knowledge companies* and consultants from whom governments are purchasing 'policy knowledge'. The UK based Matrix Knowledge Group and A4e are examples of such 'knowledge' businesses.

> The Matrix Knowledge Group has a twenty year international, national and local track record of supporting some of the biggest policy decisions by rapidly utilizing the best available evidence. Our team includes world renowned consultants, researchers, experienced practitioners, and creative software developers who collaboratively create the organisational, knowledge and information infrastructures and evidence to deliver improvements in performance and value. The team is supported by a world class, worldwide network of well-regarded partner organisations and academic advisors.
>
> (http://www.matrixknowledge.com/)

Matrix produces 'evidence-based' policy knowledge using indicators of performance and value and offers the possibilities of 'improvements' in delivery in these terms. Policy itself is rendered into a commodity in both senses. Policy solutions are for sale, and these solutions render policy into a set of measurable outcomes. When represented in this way, as a set of calculabilities, service delivery becomes 'contractable' and can be 'contracted out'. For business, there is a virtuous circle between the generation of policy knowledge, policy itself and new profit opportunities. Matrix has offices in London, Maryland, US and interestingly, given previous discussion (Chapter 3), a branch office in Hyderabad, India.

> **Matrix Knowledge India** is a subsidiary of the *Matrix Knowledge Group* and operates in India in partnership with *Mega Ace Consultancy* – India's premier economics and business incubation consultancy ... We are an Indian Company who understand what India wants, how India works and what it means to be successful.
>
> (Matrix Knowledge India website)

Such claims align discursively with the current policy rhetorics of governments seeking to make their nations more competitive in the global economy and their public services more productive and cost-effective.

As previously, the focus is upon measurement and 'results'. Similarly, A4e, a broad-based UK public service company, which now also operates in France and Germany, offers to the state 'innovation' or 'reform knowledge', and new solutions to intractable social problems. As their website asserts, they will 'Test new ways of delivering front line public services'.

> At A4e, we work with governments across the globe to 'square circles'. We tackle the difficult problems. We address market failure. We take pilot programmes and test new ways of delivering front line public services. And we deliver complex services at scale. Employing over 3100 people across 201 locations in eleven countries, we are the partner of choice for government organisations looking to deliver results.
> (http://www.mya4e.com/getdoc/45e90dbf-b4e7—4c2a-93f7—38ab844f347d/4-Governments.aspx)

In many countries education and consultancy businesses are firmly embedded in the complex, intersecting networks of policy-making and policy delivery and various kinds of *transaction* work – brokerage and contract writing, programme evaluation, legal services – much of which is hidden from view. Various kinds of 'statework' are done through multiple relationships and responsibilities in and in relation to educational governance – the businesses act as advisers, evaluators, service deliverers, philanthropists, researchers, reviewers, brokers, 'partners', committee members and as consultants and auditors. Again new policies, like England's Free Schools initiative, create new transaction business and other business opportunities.

> Three education consulting companies that worked on academy projects under Labour told the *Guardian* they had won new contracts to help set up free schools. Place Group received £1.46m in the coalition's first five months for work commissioned before the election. It has now secured contracts to work with two free schools. Appleyards received £2.9m and will support two proposed free schools, helping to develop the business case for a Montessori primary school in Crawley, West Sussex, and a Sikh free school in Birmingham. Cambridge Education was paid £1.1m for work predating the election; it will now work with a free school, the King's Science Academy in Bradford. If the government approves its business case, the consultants would arrange procedures for admissions, curriculum, staff, premises and finance.
>
> A DfE spokesman said: 'We have introduced significant restrictions on spending on consultants … so that only the most essential spending can proceed, subject to ministerial and Cabinet Office approval.' (Rachel Williams and Jeevan Vasagar, 25 November, 2010, http://www.guardian.co.uk/politics/2010/nov/19/government-data-schools-welfare-coal.)
>
> Five firms have received a total of £21 million from the Department for Education in the past year. The largest payment was £4,379,203 to

Tribal Education. A spokeswoman for the firm said: 'Tribal is currently working with one free school and three academies in a project management capacity ... Dickinson Dees, the law firm, said it had been paid to handle free school cases with building costs of £4 million in February this year'.

(Joanna Sugden, *The Times*, 27 April 2011, p. 6.)

I am going to use as an example here one company, Pricewaterhouse-Coopers LLP (PWC) in order to convey something of the extent, intensity and strategic engagement of businesses in the 'business' of education policy and education research. Three things need to be made clear. First, this account scratches the surfaces of the range and number of involvements with and in the state, even of PWC. It is limited here to education; similar lists could be developed for a whole variety of other areas of public service and state activity. Second, similar accounts could be developed for Deloitte and Touche, Ernst and Young, KPMG, McKinsey, the Hay Group, Accenture and other firms.[4] Third, the involvements listed here are taken from the period of the UK Labour governments (1997–2010) but there is every indication that the outsourcing of 'policy work' and 'state work' will increase further under the current Coalition government, although the government has pledged to cut these expenditures.

The accounts which governments give of their reforms often conflate new forms of service delivery with the work of system redesign, the creation of new infrastructures and transaction work – writing tenders, brokerage, changes to the legal status of new providers and so on.

> The government's 'Open Public Services White Paper', due in July, will set out the bold blueprint for the reform of our public services. It is a process that is not just about efficiencies, cost savings or achieving value for money. But an opportunity to rethink and reform how services are designed, to systematically engage with communities and gain a better understanding of how to integrate services and create better outcomes. Releasing services from the grip of state control encourages bids for public work from voluntary groups, charities and the private sector.
>
> (events@public-sector-events.org.uk)

PWC is the largest firm of accountants and management consultants in the United Kingdom, with over 16,000 partners and staff operating from 37 offices worldwide. PWC has multiple relationships in and with various departments and agencies of the education state at international, national, regional and local levels. They are thoroughly embedded and intertwined inside the state through their multiple roles, relationships and responsibilities (see Box 5.1) as part of loosely coupled, flexible policy-making networks. Within these diverse roles and relationships they are at different 'moments' suppliers of services, commissioners and brokers.[5]

Box 5.1 PWC and education policy work

DfES Teachers Workload study (December 2001).[1]

Academies evaluation (February 2003): an independent, five-year evaluation of the Academies initiative for the DfES.[2]

DfES Children's Services: Overarching Report on Children's Services Markets (September 2006).[3]

School workforce remodelling toolkit (2004).

Evaluation of the role of teachers in Education Action Zones for DfES (2001).

Evaluators of Lincolnshire's BIPs (Behaviour Improvement Programmes).

Westminster Local Authority advisers on BSF strategy.

Reports for DfES on impact of Capital investment on schools.

Building Performance (2001).

Building Better Performance (2003).

Wrote the out-sourcing contracts and acted as appointment broker for: Islington (CEA), Swindon (Tribal), North East Lincolnshire (Mouchell Parkman and Outcomes UK), Bradford (SERCO), LEAs and so on.

Contracted to procure strategic partner for Plymouth City Council Children's Services (CEA and OLM).

Using ITC in Schools: Addressing Teacher Workload Issues: research report no. 595 for DfES (2004).

Independent Study into School Leadership for DfES (January 2007).

Part of Education Funding Strategy Group.

QCA report *Financial Modelling of the English Examination System* (2004).

QCA's internal auditors.

Conducted for QCA the Curriculum 2000 Evaluation Survey (DfES/PWC 2004).

Evaluation report and *Report on the Future of The London Partnership* (2003), which includes a 'worked up model' of collaboration and 'explores the involvement of PWC, and other private sector organisations with the partnership in the longer term' (DfES standards website 31 July 2007).

Auditors for Darlington Borough Council and 21 other LAs – and consultant to Darlington's PFI contractor Kajima, as in Kajima's adoption of RIB financial software.

By 2003 had a PFI practice of 132 projects across the UK.

Martin Callaghan, partner in PWC Infrastructure, Government and Utilities practice, who previously managed the operational activities of Partnerships for Schools (which delivers BSF), joined the National College for School Leadership governing council in 2006.

Internal Auditors of BECTA.

Asked by BECTA to explore issues related to educational software licensing (2006).

Worked with DfES Centre for Procurement Practice and LA Regional Centre of Excellence to engage with several authorities to learn about efficiency and procurement practices introduced to deliver Change for Children reforms.

Produced with the ODPM, National Procurement Strategy and 4pS the Partnering and Procurement newsletter.

DfES and Government for London report on *The impact of mobility on service delivery to London children* (2006).

Membership of the London Child Mobility Group (Alex Chard).

Two studies part of HEFCE Equal Opportunities Research Programme 1. Cross-sectoral comparative study 2. Cross-national comparative study.

Edward Smith, a chartered accountant and a senior partner in Pricewaterhouse Coopers (PWC), appointed to the HEFCE Board (2004).

Report on a *Business Model for the e-University* for HEFCE (2000), Development for the HEFCE of a good practice guide on the effective financial management of HE institutions.

Evaluation for the CVCP (now Universities UK) of the extent of overhead recovery on research contracts with government departments.

Research report for Universities UK (2007), *The Economic Benefits of a Degree*.

Evaluation for the HEFCE of its funding method for teaching.

A project with HEFCE to develop good practice guidance for risk management in the sector.

Working with the Department for Education and Skills and HEFCE on monitoring and supporting the consortia implementing the vocationally oriented Foundation Degree.

Member LSC internal audit working group (Sarah Nattress).

Adult Learning Inspectorate – Internal auditors.

Appointed to support the LSC in developing the business requirements of the MIAP programme and to procure suppliers to design, build and operate the new services that will deliver it. Review of the DfES's relationship with UfI.

As part of their Corporate Responsibility programme PWC are involved in:

Euro-traveller Challenge – a numeracy-based learning project in partnership with British Airways and the Hillingdon business partnership with two secondary schools, as part of the London Challenge.

Partnership with VRH (Volunteer Reading Help) – 200 PWC staff became trained volunteers.

PWC is a national founding member of Cares, a BitC business-led employee volunteering programme.

Elsewhere, PWC sponsors the Russian charity Maria's Children and supports the International Finance Corporation project 'Chance for Success' and conducts special programmes at HE institutions in Moscow which help students gain practical experience in audit and consulting.

PWC (Singapore) has underwritten the costs of publishing a book documenting the learning of children from the Child at Street 11 charity.

1 PricewaterhouseCoopers worked with 100 primary, secondary, nursery and special schools across England and Wales to investigate the full range of teachers' and head teachers' jobs.

2 The aim of the evaluation is to assess the overall effectiveness of the initiative, in terms of its contribution to educational standards, and to examine the impact of key features of Academies, including sponsorship, governance, leadership and buildings.

3 The DfES contracted PricewaterhouseCoopers to produce four separate reports on five children's services markets. The markets are: Children's Homes and Fostering (two separate but very closely linked markets); Parental Positive Activities for Young People; and Childcare. The objectives of these reports are twofold: to identify the cross-cutting issues common to the markets; and to put forward suggestions for improvement as inputs into DfES policy thinking.

Here then PWC is undertaking research and evaluation, designing programmes, offering advice and making recommendations, writing and brokering outsourcing contracts, writing scoping reports, and engaging in educational philanthropy – often in relation to new policy initiatives and priorities – across all sectors of education. There are also glimpses here of the personal participation of PWC employees in policy work as members of Boards, committees and working groups, and so on (National College of School Leadership, HEFCE, Child Mobility Group, Learning and Skills Council audit group). The work of report writing and evaluation also takes PWC into the heart of the policy-making process and the processes of governance: 'face-to-face interactions in these globalizing microspaces play a central role in shaping policies and policy learning' (McCann, 2011, p. 45). Through these social interactions and report-writing, PWC also has numerous opportunities to articulate a view of the public sector and public services generally. That view often takes the form of a critique of state provision and providers and arguments for the advantages of contracting out or the creation of service markets – as is evident in the examples. In one sense we can see this as the 'apparently mundane' work of neo-liberalism, extending the role of 'the private' and commodifying even more the social and the public domain. These involvements and recommendations also in a variety of ways act back on the state itself, changing the landscape of the state, its self-organisation, and repeopling it with those 'in the conversation'. As a result, the boundaries between state, economy and civil society become increasingly blurred; and there is a new mix within the matrix of governance involving 'complex relations of reciprocal interdependence' (Jessop, 2002, p. 52) between business and the state. These companies are used by governments as a policy device, a way of trying things out, getting things done, changing things, and avoiding established public sector lobbies and interests, in an attempt to 'routinise innovation' and incubate creative possibilities (Thrift, 2005, p. 7). They can serve to 'short-circuit' or displace existing policy blockages. PWC and other firms also bring to bear a range of simple but 'effective' techniques of governance onto and into the work of policy, as Larner suggests: 'Best practice, audit, contracts, performance indicators, and benchmarks are all techniques worthy of geographical atten-tion' (Larner, 2003, p. 511). New sorts of professions and professional knowledge become important in all of this: 'the rise of knowledge-based professions and the brokering of knowledge by knowledge managers are both central in making post-bureaucracy "happen"' (Grek & Ozga, 2010).

Neo-liberalism is bottom-up as well as top-down. That is, as Larner puts it, we need to see 'neoliberalism as involving processes that produce spaces, states, and subjects in complex and multiple forms ... Indeed, it may be more useful to think of particular spaces, states, and subjects as artefacts, rather than as architects, of neoliberalism' (Larner, 2003).

Two sorts of 'governing knowledge' are being traded here. The first kind takes the form of or is represented in numbers, as evaluations, comparisons and rankings of public sector organisations, and is what might be called *'knowledge about'* – although this is not simply a means of describing, it is an effective knowledge; through processes of performativity it organises that which it describes. The second kind is *'knowledge for'*, which takes the form of discourse and practices as methods of organisation or means of reform of public sector actors – involving changes to their form, their culture and their conduct, reflexive organisational redesign. These two forms of knowl-edge, and the work of organisational calibration and improvement, were also evident in the previous account of retail edu-businesses, and again they are generic. This is what Rizvi and Lingard (2010, p. 118) describe as 'the ecumenical move of private-sector structures and practices inside state structures'.

Companies like PWC, as noted, operate on a global scale. They and other consultants and education service companies are eager to 'export' their 'products' and policy knowledge, and take up the opportunities of reform processes and public sector 'modernisation' in countries around the world. This is the third layer of policy work and privatisation.

Exporting and 'selling' policy: a global market in policy ideas

There is now an extensive global flow of policy knowledge in the field of education. As noted already, Cambridge Education, which is a UK edu-business, a subsidiary of Mott Macdonald (see Chapter 6), is active in the USA and has worked in over 60 other countries. Cambridge has been or is currently working with, among others:

National Government of Thailand
Provincial governments in China
Education Ministry in Hong Kong
California
New Orleans
City of New York
DfiD, EC, Word Bank, ADB projects in Papua New Guinea, Eritrea, Bangladesh, Cambodia and so on.

Cambridge also works in partnership with universities, NGOs and other private companies and is involved in a range of projects with the Gates Foundation. Among its policy 'products' it offers versions of the English school inspection model to other countries. Cambridge did hold a national contract for school inspection work in England. New York City, Thailand and Beijing have all 'bought' this model.

New York, the US's largest school district, with 1.1m students, has hired Cambridge Education to lead the introduction of a programme of 'school reviews' based on the English Inspections model (worth around $6.4m a year). CE is an Inspection contractor in England. CE is training New York reviewers so that they can assume full control of the review system in coming years. As the tabloid *New York Sun* put it 'The British have arrived: They're reviewing city schools' (31 July 2007).

School Assessment/Inspections: Cambridge Education supports the Thai Office for National Education Standards and Quality Assessment (ONESQA) with the enhancement of educational quality in Thailand through the provision of trained school assessors nationwide. Over the past ten years, ONESQA has been implementing a programme of school inspections/assessment to ensure equal standards in schools across Thailand and to improve the quality of education nationally. Cambridge Education provides teams of trained and experienced assessors to undertake inspections of educational institutions in basic education schools and adult institutions throughout Thailand. The teams are trained by senior staff at Cambridge Education. Using appropriate assessment methods and tools which are in compliance with ONESQA requirements, the assessors provide useful recommendations to the schools to support continuous quality assurance and the enhancement of educational quality. School Evaluation Reports for each school that is quality controlled by the Cambridge Education office teams are submitted to both the schools and ONESQA.

(Cambridge website).

Here experience, knowledge and expertise gained in the English education services market is repackaged, sold and exported, often without much attention being given to the risks and problems associated with the policies or models involved. Holden (2009, p. 321) makes this point in his discussion of the export of the UK's public–private partnership and private finance initiative models. The problems, debates and controversies which have accompanied the use of PFIs, in particular in the UK, are erased when such schemes are sold to other countries – Holden's account focuses specifically on sales to Eastern Europe, China, India and Chile:

> ... the PPP/PFI policy has been extremely controversial in the UK and its benefits and drawbacks have been vigorously debated. It is possible that the drawbacks of PPP/PFI may be accentuated for developing countries as a result of severe resource constraints, locking them into long-term arrangements which may divert resources from elsewhere. PPP/PFI appears to release more resources in the short-term, but entails expensive commitments in the long-term, and cannot be renegotiated by the public sector without huge penalties. The apparent transfer of risk to the private sector may be even more illusory in developing countries than in developed countries, where technical know-how and the administrative capacity to enforce rigorous contracts with private sector providers may be lacking.
>
> (Holden, 2009, p. 321)

Nonetheless, the 'testing' and 'development' of products in the contexts of UK education reforms is often presented as a selling point to new clients.

> The UK experience has served as the underlying model for much of the development internationally of SBM [School Based Management].
>
> (www.cea.co.uk)

> Nord Anglia's reputation and expertise with British education gives it a rare opportunity to capitalise upon the demand in overseas markets for improved quality in education provision.
>
> (Company Annual Report 2006, p. 8)

A further example of the export of UK policy ideas is the work of consultant and policy entrepreneur Michael Barber, one time Head of the Prime Minister's Delivery Unit (2001–5), latterly Head of McKinsey's global education practice (see Figure 5.1; see also Chapter 6). His big policy idea,

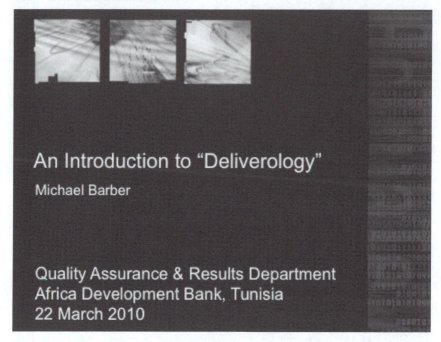

Figure 5.1 Michael Barber: PowerPoint presentation.

developed during his work under New Labour and explained in his book *Instruction to Deliver* (Barber, 2007), is now for sale as part of McKinsey's suite of management products and is presented as a generic policy solution to public sector effectiveness to agencies and governments around the world.

The UK government is eager to support foreign-currency earning activities like PFI, and as Holden (2009) goes on to suggest, in this global knowledge economy the substantive benefits or dangers to the recipient countries are less important to the UK government than is the material interest of the companies doing the 'selling'. This is an 'export strategy' rather than a development strategy – although 'developing country governments may request some form of aid as the price for adopting the model being sold to them' (Holden, 2009, p. 328).

Companies like Cambridge are keen to expand and are looking for new market opportunities. Cambridge has recently opened offices in Australia, working with a local private education services provider, Teacher Training Australia.

> TTA and Cambridge Education team up in Australia
> Cambridge Education has expanded its education capability in Australia through a strategic alliance with education specialist Teacher Training Australia (TTA). This alliance is another step towards

consolidating Cambridge Education and parent company Mott MacDonald's presence in Australia, and follows the acquisition of Australian firm Hughes Trueman.... TTA is an independent Australian organisation established to provide high quality professional development courses for Australian teachers, using an innovative, practitioner-led model. Since forming in 2005 it has run over 500 courses across all curriculum areas with participants from all educational sectors, at both primary and secondary school level. The company is currently working in New South Wales, Victoria and Queensland.... Cambridge Education will work to develop the alliance's presence in Australia – for both TTA and Cambridge Education developed services and products – and to open new markets for TTA's approach overseas.... Richard Birch, Cambridge Education's retiring managing director, will move to Australia next year to focus on this new business. He welcomes the alliance: 'TTA have an excellent track record facilitating the delivery of teacher developed professional development. They share Cambridge Education's aim to provide high quality, practical services for our clients. Together we can offer a unique range of services in the Australian education sector and further afield.'

> (http://www.camb-ed.com/Home/News/
> TTAandCambridgeEducation.aspx)

Cambridge Education Australia also recently qualified with the Bastow Institute of Educational Leadership in Victoria, to deliver programmes in General Leadership, Coaching and Mentoring, Early Childhood and Development and has gained a prequalification to provide consultancy services to the New South Wales Government in areas such as Performance Review, Service Delivery Improvement and Organisational Capacity.

Cambridge is also involved in various national settings in writing education policy, particularly for small states, as explained on the company website:

> Our services are comprehensive: from assisting with education policy development and advising on education financing, through programme and project design and management, to social and institutional development. We have considerable **expertise** in capacity building, helping to form solid foundations for education development and reform. We provide technical assistance and training in all aspects of education – for example in developing curriculum and learning materials, and training teachers.

> (Company website, accessed 8 October 2010)

For example, the Asian Development Bank has paid Cambridge Education to:

> support ... the Maldives in drafting legislation for a new Education Act; in developing a sustainable financial framework for increased and

equitable access to post-secondary education; and in enhancing capacity
to develop learning and teaching materials for lower secondary grades.
(http://www.camb-ed.com/International/internationalprojects/
internationalcountries/MaldivesStrengtheningtheFrameworkof
Education/tabid/172/Default.aspx, accessed 8 October 2010)

Here the company is not just an adviser or consultant; it is *writing*
education policy first hand and inducting local politicians and civil servants
into the practices and perspectives of Western policy and policy-making.
Here the privatisation of policy is at its most direct. Again we see the
commodification of education policy knowledge. Knowledge and experience
are sold with the effect of moving policies, policy concepts and languages
between national settings, mostly from west to east and north to south.
However, companies based in India, like NIIT, and Japan, like Benesse
(with offices in Hong Kong, Korea and Taiwan), and others from Australia
and New Zealand, are now expanding into this international trade in
policies, policy ideas and educational services. Again these activities signal
the participation of new knowledge brokers within policy conversations and
a global convergence in forms of institutional and state governance based on
transnational knowledges (Grek et al., 2009).

Giving yourself away

Business philanthropy and business relationships also provide conduits
for the international mobility of generic policy ideas, and means for the
insinuation of particular forms of knowledge and types of relationship inside
the state for representatives of business. Business philanthropies can act
as national and international policy brokers.

An example of the export of reform ideas through philanthropic activity is
Partnerships for Learning – Deutschland (PfL). The PfL programme was
developed from a London pilot in 1996 initiated by the accountancy and
consultancy firm KPMG, working with the Business in the Community
(BitC) charity. Since its UK launch, 5,000 head teachers have been matched
with a business partner. Over 1,200 companies throughout the United
Kingdom have been involved. KPMG also participated in the extension
of this programme in Germany, together with companies like Herlitz,
Deutsche Bank and Siemens. It provides mentoring support to head teachers
in Berlin, Brandenburg and Frankfurt. Since 2005, altogether 86 schools
have registered for the German scheme.

Another example of the mobility of policy ideas via networks of business
philanthropy is the Teach First programme (see also Chapter 4). This origi-
nated in the USA as Teach for America and was imported into England as
Teach First (TF); it is a teacher training and recruitment programme aimed
at placing graduates from elite universities in socially disadvantaged schools
for two years (although in England around 60 per cent of participations now

stay on beyond their initial two year commitment). TF (which is supported by a mix of corporate and government funding) is now the largest single graduate recruiter from Oxford and Cambridge and it is being exported globally through Teach for All (see website for funders) to countries including Germany, Estonia, Latvia, India, Australia, Lebanon and Chile. TF brings new concepts and language into teacher education programmes and has received high-level political support in the US, UK and the importing countries.

A final example of international links and movements comes from a business philanthropy network established by the Private Equity Foundation (PEF), a UK-based private equity and venture capital funded charity, which now also operates in Germany through the Forum for Active Philanthropy and recently made its first 'investment' in the Hamburger Hauptschul-modell (HHM). This is a charity helping young people in the transition from school to work. PEF is looking to expand further and in France is currently working with the KPMG France Foundation 'to learn more about the charity landscape and identify organizations that we may be able to work with' (PEF website).

Germany provides an interesting example of a national philanthropic foundation which is taking on responsibilities for the reform and reflexive redesign of public sector schools which would previously have been held by Länder. The Bertelsmann Stiftung (The Bertelsmann Foundation of Germany) claim in their strap line that they are 'Inspiring People. Shaping the Future' (see Figure 5.2).

Bertelsmann are doing the work of education reform in Germany and doing policy, again bringing now familiar knowledges and techniques to bear, working with and inside the state.

> The Bertelsmann Stiftung has been working to improve quality in schools and the education system since the 1990s. We at the foundation believe that efforts to improve schools and teaching need to focus on three key elements: greater autonomy for schools, systematic evaluation processes and effective support systems for the schools. The Bertelsmann Stiftung is working together with education authorities from North Rhine-Westphalia, Lower Saxony and Baden-Württemberg on pilot projects testing and expanding school autonomy in regional education networks.
>
> (Company website)

The sorts of techniques and programmes they offer again focus on knowledges *about* and knowledges *for*, the improvement and calibration couplet discussed earlier. From the Bertelsmann website you can choose your policy, place it in your 'shopping cart' and order it online (see Figure 5.2). Visually, here, policy products are no different from other commodities that can be bought online.

Figure 5.2 Bertelsmann Stiftung.

A convergence of governance

As noted already, these new forms of participation in the provision, monitoring and evaluation of public sector services, and new forms of public sector organisation, bring new players, voices, values and discourses into policy conversations. In effect, to different extents in different countries, the private sector now occupies a range of roles and relationships within the state and the educational state in particular, as sponsors and benefactors, as well as working as contractors, consultants, advisers, researchers, service providers and so on, and both sponsoring innovations (by philanthropic action) *and* selling policy solutions and services to the state, sometimes in related ways. Education policy communities are thus being reconstituted and new policy discourses and narratives now flow through them. New forms of policy influence are enabled and some established policy actors and agencies like educational researchers and local authorities are marginalised or disenfranchised or circumvented. In particular the new participants in the policy process colonise the spaces opened up by the critique of existing state organisations. In other words, the market in 'governing knowledges' is closely entwined with the dissemination of new policy narratives and the discrediting of older ones within the developing market in public services. This is indicative of a new 'architecture of regulation' based on interlocking relationships between disparate sites in and beyond the state and displays many of the characteristics of what Richards and Smith (2002, pp. 28–36) call a 'postmodern state'. The participants in these new, diverse and disaggregated policy communities act from many 'points' and sites, roles and responsibilities, which constitute a new grid of power 'above, across, as well as within, state boundaries' (Cerny, 1997, p. 253) through which particular forms of discourse are distributed, embedded and naturalised. Commercial consultants and public service companies (as well as philanthropists of various kinds) are eager to provide and enact radical and innovative 'solutions' to policy problems, solutions which almost always take the form of inserting into public sector organisations technologies of 'modernisation' and 'transformation' and metagovernance (like leadership, performativity, marketisation) as well as changing the relations between organisations – as in the deployment of the 'market form', but also via the development of partnerships, consortia and contracting. However, in many instances, as part of the process of reform, public service companies are seeking to replace state providers by becoming public service contractors.

Both the aspects and planes of neo-liberalism, discussed in Chapter 1, the economic and the governmental, are evident here and are tightly intertwined. Business is both a beneficiary of and a method of reform – either in replacing public sector providers or working to change the subjectivities, practices and discourses of these providers. The state is also remaking itself in these terms – and is both an object of suspicion and a subject of reform. It is making itself smaller and more strategic. Although different in form, the two sorts of reforming knowledge (*about* and *for*) are intimately connected at the level of organisational functioning; both are moral technologies focused on teachers as 'practical subjects', they activate teachers and researchers towards 'productive' ends. As indicated already, they work in very mundane ways through specific techniques, like annual reviews, appraisals, 'goal-setting, tests and a number of new comprehensive and mandatory reporting mechanisms' (Andersen, Dahler-Larsen & Pedersen, 2009) and so on, and the insertion of generic commercial relations based on contracts, best value, partnerships, performance monitoring, brokering and so on. These, in their component parts and as a whole, constitute a political economy of details (Foucault, 1979, p. 139) which play their small parts in the more general processes of 'diffusion of the neoliberal doxa' (Wacquant, 1999).

> These relationships take the form of a multiplicity of often minor processes, of different origin and scattered location across and beyond the state. These overlap, repeat, or imitate one another according to their domain of application, they converge and gradually produce the blueprint of a general method.
>
> (Foucault, 1979, p. 138)

Within all of this, 'reform' ideas or forms of 'improvement' which seemed radical, even unthinkable, become more and more possible, then normal and then necessary – in part through what I call a 'ratchet effect' (Ball, 2008b). Over time, practices that are 'fragmented, repetitive and discontinuous' (Foucault, 2004, p. 4) become 'totally inscribed in general and essential transformations' (Foucault, 1979, p. 139). In this case in the *'firming-up'* or *enterprising* of the public sector, and indeed of the state itself.

All of this is not entirely new; restless capital is always seeking new opportunities for profit, new possibilities for commodification! Especially at times when other arenas of profit are less attractive. Here though there is an iterative relationship between policy change, policy opportunities created by the state, for knowledge and services, and policy solutions which are sold by the private sector to the state, in the form of consultation *reports and recommendations* for the reform of the state itself and of the public sector, and such reforms once implemented (as in the case of marketisation of services) in turn create new opportunities for profit for private sector organisations.

Also, as indicated in previous chapters, there are points of imbrication between edu-business and critics and criticisms of state education. To the extent that public sector education can be represented as 'broken' then there is more 'fixing' for the private sector to do. As Saltman (2007, p. 119) puts it, 'natural and unnatural disasters have been used for the radical social and economic engineering of schooling by the political Right'. The practical work of re-engineering is profitable. While the state is the key market maker here, as Peck (2003, p. 228) suggests, this kind of policy mobility and emulation has been 'speeded-up' by 'the explosive growth of "policy intermediation" institutions since the 1970s (such as think tanks, policy networks and centers, reform advocates and consultants), the modus operandi of which is defined in terms of the generation, circulation and implantation of potentially agenda-shifting ideas models and strategies'. Furthermore, Peet (2000) suggests that London is one of a number of 'centers of persuasion' in a neo-liberal ideological-discursive project and that such persuasion is very material as well as very ideological. Business is seeking profit.

> Consultancies and their knowledge claims are undoubtedly an important component of the process, yet the strategy is not driven primarily by these knowledge claims or even by the wider ideology within which these are situated. Direct material interests are evidently the key explanatory factor.
>
> (Holden, 2009, p. 330)

In education, policy transfer, policy colonisation and policy convergence are all being effected here, through the writing of policy, policy consultancy and recommendations, policy influence, the selling of management and improvement products, and the growth and spread of multinational service providers with standardised methods and contents at various levels of policy. New policy relationships and spaces and media are constituted and used to re-embed mobile policies and their attendant discourses in national territories. Concomitantly, public services are being redesigned or modernised (see Ball, 2008a) to meet the needs of the neo-liberal state, although, at the same time, national governments, especially those of small and fragile states, may be experiencing a reduction in their capacity to steer their education systems (see also Dale, 2006). Through all of this, and despite the interpretation and modification of policy products at national and local levels (which I have not attended to here) there is clearly now something we can call 'global education policy' – a generic set of concepts, language and practices that is recognisable in various forms and is for sale!

Notes

1 At this stage I am using the term MNEB loosely and as a catch-all to identify a set of trends in global education policy-making. Further work is needed to bring greater precision and differentiation to this diverse and highly dynamic business sector, as I did previously with UK edu-businesses (Ball, 2007). The intention is that the examples given will provide some clarity. But here I am seeking to sketch out a new policy terrain and identify a set of policy mobilities, within which MNEBs are key players.

2 I am grateful to Patricia Burch for emphasising this point to me.

3 All the quotations used come from company brochures or website documents and these were accessed during 2005 – for examples of full documents see:
http://www.cocentra.info/gateway/uploads/panda%20leaflet.pdf
http://www.edisonschools.co.uk/
http://www.prospects.co.uk/data_page.asp?pageID=97=4

4 'KPMG is committed to helping shape education at both the local and national level. We are involved in both policy discussions and implementation to ensure that employability issues are well represented' (Mike Rake, Chairman of KPMG International and Senior Partner of KPMG in the UK). KPMG is co-sponsor with the City of London Corporation of an Academy, and a supporter of Every Child a Reader.

5 As an exercise in policy ethnography I undertook two days of paid consultancy for PWC, contributing to the writing of a bid for a National Audit Office contract. The speed, efficiency and intellectual standard of the discussions and writing were, I have to say, impressive. Very little of what I wrote appeared in the final bid document. PWC did not win the tender.

6 Education as big business

This chapter moves on from where the last left off. Here we look again into the world of multinational edu-business and begin to explore the buying and selling of education services, and materials and educational institutions, and the relationships of these activities to the general dynamics of business growth, business performance and profitability. Again this will be discussed in relation to the implications for education policy, although in this case from the perspective of corporate strategy, corporate finance and private equity investment. There are three sections to the chapter. First, some examples of corporate consolidations and private equity purchases related to edu-business will be explored. Second, the corporate growth and global scope of Pearson Education, the world's largest edu-business, will be outlined. Third, I will look at the 'commercialisation' and 'privatisation' of British universities, and others, as they involve themselves in 'for-profit' offshore campus ventures in South-East Asia, and the increasingly convoluted relations between 'public' universities and private higher education companies.

Consolidations and mergers

Businesses are bought and sold for a variety of reasons. In some instances the primary assets of interest are forms of so-called soft capital, that is patents, licences, market share, name brand, research staffs, methods, customer base, or culture. That is the case (primarily) in the first two sets of examples discussed in this chapter. In the third set of examples there is a mix of soft and hard capital assets involved. Furthermore, as signalled above, education as an area of business is affected by strategic decisions intended to enhance competitive advantage, create new sources of value and improve revenue growth. Such decision-making leads to vertical and horizontal integration and diversification through mergers and acquisitions. Edu-businesses are subject to the same market and business processes as other companies and there has been a series of significant acquisitions and mergers in this field in the past five years. These take two forms. One, in which Pearson is the paradigm case, is the building of big education and information conglomerates. The other is the swallowing up of edu-businesses by generic professional and management services companies, as we shall see. In these latter cases the education services divisions in these companies sit alongside housing, transport, defence and other specialist divisions and operate in the same way, often using generic methods and 'products'. These generic companies are typically based on synergies involving design, build, management and support for public sector services. The other dynamic in relation to edu-business is the growing interest in this area from private equity. That is, investments and acquisitions undertaken by private equity firms or venture capital firms, each with their own set of goals, preferences and investment strategies. They inject working capital into a target company to nurture expansion, new product development, or the restructuring of the company's operations, management or ownership, although in some cases are interested in the assets rather than the business itself.

Within all of this, then, *vertical integration* takes two forms, business activities which address markets in curriculum, pedagogy and assessment services (and support and administrative services, e.g. recruitment, payroll, budget management), and markets in different education sectors, from preschool to higher education, and vocational and professional education (e.g. Pearson). *Horizontal integration* takes the form of the development of generic business approaches which cut across professional and management services of various kinds (e.g. Mouchel Parkman and VT) and information and business information services. In the case of private equity, individual businesses are normally maintained separately as part of a diverse portfolio (see John Bauer).

Ownership!

As these business dynamics play out they raise new sorts of questions about national and foreign ownership of educational 'assets' that could have implications in terms of the ability of national governments to exert policy control over and regulate their education systems. Sweden is an interesting case in point. Sweden now has about 20 per cent of its school students educated in state-funded 'free schools', most of which are owned and run by private providers. There are 900 such schools with approximately 80,000 students from 1 to 18 years. The largest group of these schools is run by John Bauer, with upper secondary schools in 20 locations, specialising in vocational education and training such as IT, media, entrepreneurship, health and physical, hotel management and catering. The John Bauer upper secondary schools have around 10,000 students from 16 to 19 years and almost 1,000 employees. Aside from the Swedish schools, John Bauer runs international schools in Spain, hotel and catering colleges in India and Norway, and has other educational ventures in China and Tanzania, and property development activities in Central America and Indo-China. In 2007, the company had a turnover of SEK 757 million. In 2009,

John Bauer was bought by Denmark's largest private equity company, Axcel, which then had investments valued at DKK 14 billion. Axcel's other main areas of investment are in housing, fashion and pet foods.[1] Following the purchase of John Bauer (JBO) Axcel announced:

> As part of the strategy for JBO's continued development, Axcel plans to extend and strengthen the company's general management and board. In realizing this strategy, the first move has been to appoint Alf Johansson as chairman of the board of directors. Johansson is the former director of Proffice, one of the largest recruitment companies in Scandinavia with a turnover of approximately SEK 4 billion.
>
> (http://axcel.customers.composite.net/content/us/media/ 2008/axcel_acquires_jbo_in_sweden)

In 2010 another of the Swedish free school companies, AcadeMedia, was bought by EQT after a stock-market battle, with EQT outbidding rivals Providence Equity Partners. The EQT offer valued AcadeMedia at €260m. AcadeMedia is the largest general education company in Sweden with operations spanning pre- and compulsory school, upper secondary school and adult education. The company operates more than 150 schools and adult education units across Sweden and has approximately 2,500 employees and 45,000 students. EQT, the private equity arm of Sweden's Wallenberg family, is a group of private equity funds with an extremely diverse investment portfolio focused in Northern and Eastern Europe, Asia and the US. Providence Equity Partners is a US private equity investor which in 2009 bought Study Group, an Australian-based global private education provider, for $570m. Study Group has 38 campuses and 55,000 students in the UK, Australia, New Zealand and the USA. Among other things, Study Group runs International Study Centres in partnership with UK universities on their campuses, for example at Lincoln and Kingston. 'Providence is the world's leading private equity firm focused on media, communications, information and education investments. The firm manages funds with $23 billion in commitments and has invested in more than 100 companies globally since its inception in 1989' (company website). Alongside Study Group, the firm's current education industry investments include Archipelago Learning, Ascend Learning, Catalpa, Edline, and Education Management Corporation. In July 2011 Providence added to their education portfolio with the purchase of Washington-based Blackboard Inc. for $1.64 billion. Blackboard works with schools, colleges, companies, government and the military around the world.

> Blackboard works with our clients to develop and implement technology that improves every aspect of education. We enable clients to engage more students in exciting new ways, reaching them on their

terms and devices—and connecting more effectively, keeping students informed, involved, and collaborating together.

(Company website)

Ascend Learning, one of Providence's other investments, is an urban charter school company currently operating in New York. Its president and founder is Steven F. Wilson, who is also a senior fellow at Education Sector,[2] a Washington think tank, and formerly worked at the John F. Kennedy School of Government at Harvard. He is the former CEO of Advantage Schools,[3] an urban school management company that educates nearly 10,000 students in charter schools, and a former executive vice president of Edison Schools. Previously, Wilson was special assistant for strategic planning for Massachusetts Governor William Weld and co-executive director of the Pioneer Institute,[4] where he wrote the Massachusetts charter school law. He is the author of two books, *Learning on the Job: When Business Takes on Public Schools* and *Reinventing the Schools: A Radical Plan for Boston*. He is the board president of Building Excellent Schools, a national training programme for aspiring charter school founders. Wilson's biography offers a glimpse of the complex ways in which ideas, policies, enterprise and money are interlinked. It also sidelights ways in which education policy work is being 'done' in a multiplicity of new sites 'tied together on the basis of alliance and the pursuit of economic and social outcomes' (Mackenzie & Lucio, 2005, p. 500) and the evolution and ambition of private sector and third sector 'educators' and the development of alternative infrastructures for public service provision or what Wolch (1990) called 'the shadow state'. This shadow state is taking on more and more of the roles previously limited to public sector organisations and to the state itself through involvements in delivery, dialogue and decision-making. Again in this example we can see the importance of the interconnections – the networks – of policy, of business and neo-liberal ideology and practice and the flow of ideas and opportunities between them. Within these networks, as before, we can also see the practical interplay between roll-back (critique of public sector education) and roll-out (new business opportunities in public services) neo-liberalism. We can note again the significance of policy entrepreneurship, and the emergence of nodal, hybrid policy actors who, within network relations, move between politics, advocacy, public service and business and who thus play their part in what Harrison and Wood (1999) call 'manipulated emergence' – the development of new policy in the relationships between stakeholder interests and state incentives (see below).

Joining up the world of business

The UK edu-business sector is different from that of Sweden and, at the moment, is focused more on support services, consultancy and outsourcing work (see Ball, 2007 for an overview), although the private sector owns and runs a significant proportion of preschool provision and post-compulsory vocational training provision. Nonetheless, large-scale business developments and growth strategies do have a significant bearing upon edu-businesses in the UK – bear with me here! In 2007 Babcock International, a global engineering and support services company (with a turnover in 2006 of £836m), formed a joint venture with Mouchel Parkman, a business process outsourcing company with its own education services division, which provided services for individual schools, groups of schools and local authorities, as well as local authority support for the Labour government's 'Every Child Matters' agenda; it had a turnover in 2008 of £656m. The joint venture created Mpb Education, a full-service education and building services company. Among its other activities, in 2007 Mpb was named preferred bidder by the London Borough of Hackney to deliver its £167 million Building Schools for the Future (BSF) programme. Also in 2007, Mouchel bought Hyder Business Services, with its education division (heavily involved in CPD, back-office work and outsourcing), for £46.24 million, from private equity firm Terra Firma, to add to its trio of other 2006 acquisitions worth a total value of £50 million – project management and organisational change specialist Hornagold and Hills, water and utilities consultancy Ewan Group plc, and software and system solutions company Traffic Support Limited (TSL). In February 2010 the VT group, with its own education services division VTES (Vosper Thornycroft Education and Skills), which was heavily involved in careers advice, consultancy and work-based learning, and a partner in 4S, a joint venture CPD company, with Surrey Local Authority, launched a £330m bid to buy Mouchel. Almost immediately Babcock announced a £1.29bn offer for VT, but on the stipulation that it drop its bid for Mouchel. In March 2010 Babcock and VT agreed a £1.3bn merger. These various education services divisions are now consolidated as Babcock 4S, which at Babcock sits alongside its other divisions and activities. In 2010, Babcock 4S was named winner of the 'Supplier to the education sector' award, by educational publisher *Education Investor*. The award judges described Babcock 4S as 'Quite simply the most innovative school improvement service in the UK'. Babcock 4S – 'partners in education' – explains on its website:

> Our vision is to be the most innovative and high-quality education services organisation nationally, and then internationally.
>
> We partner with local authorities, schools, Academies and central government to deliver improved outcomes and reduced costs. Our services include a comprehensive CPD and events programme, a wide range of school support and development services, integrated education services in partnership with selected local authorities such as Surrey County Council and Waltham Forest Council and regional / national programmes including the Advanced Skills Teacher National Assessment Agency.
>
> (Babcock 4S website)

Like other edu-businesses Babock looks to education policy for new business opportunities.

> We can support your school through the process of becoming an Academy. We can provide as much or as little expertise as you need – from guidance on aspects of conversion to managing the whole process on your behalf. Once established as an Academy, we offer bespoke packages of support services and expertise. For our existing customers that are considering conversion to academy status, we are able to provide peace of mind and continuity of service throughout the conversion period and once established as an academy, with our bespoke academies package. We also support groups developing Free Schools, bringing together our expertise in establishing and running schools of all phases, providing as much or as little expertise as you need. We also offer bespoke packages of ongoing support services and expertise, tailored to the requirements of individual Free Schools.
>
> (Babcock 4S website)

Yet another version of these processes of business consolidation, with a twist, is evident in the example of the company 3Es. 3Es was a 'spinout company' initially owned by the Kingshurst CTC Trust. Kingshurst was England's first City Technology College,[5] founded in Birmingham in 1988. 3Es was founded by Kingshurst's first head teacher, Valerie Bragg, and was responsible for the formation of the Kingshurst Foundation – a confederation of eight schools run by the 3Es company. The initial schools in this Federation with Kingshurst were King's College, Guildford and Kings International College, Camberley. These were reopened 'failing schools' which had been outsourced by Surrey Local Authority to 3Es to manage. Later the Bexley Business Academy was added to the Federation and in 2003 Valerie Bragg became Executive Head of the Academy as well as project manager of academies in Slough and Bristol, and elsewhere, often in collaboration with Foster and Partners, Architects. Valerie Bragg was also a member of Prince Philip's think tank on national and international issues from 1990 to 2004 and under New Labour an adviser to the Prime Minister's office on the regeneration of schools, a specialist adviser to the House of Commons Select Committee on Education and Skills, an OfSTED inspector and chair of RIBA Design Quality Forum for Schools. She was also part of a consortium bidding for a Building Schools for the Future contract in Burnley. In 2009 she, with colleagues, launched a charitable trust, Innovative Schools, which is proposing to establish a chain of 20–30 new non-selective maintained academies. However, in 2006 3Es was acquired by Faber Maunsell, a UK consulting-engineering company. In 2009 Faber Maunsell became a subsidiary of California-based Aecom Technology Corporation, with approximately 46,000 employees around the world, which works in transportation, planning and design, building engineering, government services, environment, water, energy and power, and programme management, and currently holds two major contracts with the US Defence Department for security and reconstruction work in Iraq.

> AECOM National Security Program
>   Iraq Counter Intelligence and Human Intelligence Careers
>   Discover an exciting and rewarding career with National Security Programs, that builds on your experience supporting the U.S. Government in its ongoing efforts to rebuild Iraq. Learn more about these career opportunities and other opportunities with AECOM's National Security Programs Division. Visit www.nsp-aecom.com or contact your recruiter for further information.
>   We are seeking Military Analysts, as well as Iraqi-born Special Advisors, Senior Advisors and Iraqi-born Americans who are fluent speakers of Arabic and dialects commonly found throughout Iraq.
>
> • Provide an understanding of the complex issues across Iraq …
> • Assist America's troops with situational awareness …
> • Share the attitudes, perceptions and living conditions of the Iraqi people.
>   (http://humanintelcareers.com/careers/iraq-cihumint-careers/)

In 2010 AECOM was awarded a five-year, $US53-million contract from the US Agency for International Development (USAID) to provide economic-consulting services to Iraq through the Iraq Financial Sector Development Program. Valerie Bragg is now a director and Head of the Education Sector at 3Es AECOM. Like Steve Wilson, Valerie Bragg is a hybrid, mobile, heterarchical actor moving between and joining up third sector, public sector and business sector organisations around business opportunities (academies, BSF, outsourcing and so on). She is head teacher, policy adviser, consultant and businesswoman. She discursively and symbolically carries neo-liberal policy messages and knowledges into government, participates in new forms of governance and embodies the entrepreneurial spirit. In both cases these actors get neo-liberalism 'done' in education.

As a final example of the merging and globalizing of edu-business, in 2007 Edison Schools and Global Education Management Systems (GEMS) announced an International Alliance. New York-based Edison Schools is the largest manager of US and UK public schools (see Saltman, 2005, and recall the links with Wilson and Pioneer above), and Dubai-based GEMS is the largest private school operator in the Middle East, China and India. The new partnership intends to build a network of private schools with campuses in major cities around the world. Edison Schools also licensed its intellectual property and brand to GEMS for the management of public schools in the

Middle East, North Africa and Southern Asia. The respective company founders said in a joint statement:

> We believe that great pedagogy is portable; that educational quality is enhanced by international collaboration; and that organisations like those we have founded will be increasing and positive contributors to both public and private schools worldwide.
>
> (http://www.businesswire.com/news/home/20070109005769/en/ Edison-Schools-Global-Education-Management-Systems-Announce)

Edison Schools was founded in 1992, enrols more than 285,000 public school students in 19 US states, and the United Kingdom. It employs approximately 6,000 full-time workers. GEMS manages approximately 100 private schools, some dating back 40 years, in the UAE, England, India, and other countries with a total enrolment of over 70,000 students. GEMS employs over 6,000 educational professionals and provides education for children of more than 100 nationalities.

Each of these examples, in different but related ways, indicates something of the degree of interest in education by business, and the size and value of the various global markets in education services, but they only scratch the surface. They also illustrate the global form of edu-business in terms of ownership and reach. Here we see the growth, through acquisitions and mergers, of global education brands which market standard services, products and policy solutions in diverse national settings and which in some cases wield considerable financial influence in relation to education policy. Put simply, there are three sorts of companies – specialist (like GEMS and Edison, although GEMs also operates in health care), generic (like Babcock and Mott Macdonald, parent company of Cambridge Education), and portfolio (the private equity investors like Providence and Axcel and KKR – see below). Pearson, discussed below, cuts across these categories. In the generic companies education services divisions sit alongside other divisions – transport, housing, energy and so on. They are integrated in relation to both soft and hard service provision, professional and managerial services and accountancy on the one hand, building, design and engineering on the other. In relation to education, the business logic, especially in the UK, has been a fairly direct response to and engagement with education policy developments. Under New Labour, the Academies (see Ball, 2007) and Building Schools for the Future programmes opened up massive opportunities for new work in school design, engineering and construction, project design and school management, alongside the out-sourcing of education programmes and retail services (discussed in the previous chapter). The portfolio companies normally run their education businesses separately and alongside other different kinds of investments, although Providence does have a focused strategy around education as an area of investment. Providence is also interested in different educational media – both face-to-face fixed educational services and virtual IT-based services.

There are some latent political issues embedded in these developments in terms of the relationship of ownership to policy, both in terms of policy influence and the alignments and misalignments between company and national interests, as well as, in some cases, the opacity of ownership, and change of ownership and the disconnects between brand and ownership. As yet we have little sense of the significance of the foreign ownership of national educational infrastructure or services and the limits that this may place on national policy options or the possibility that multinational education businesses will use their leverage to influence national policies in their interest or the possible impact of business failures for national governments.

However, these businesses and the nodal actors, discussed above, who work in relation to them, do play their part in the 'purposeful' destatalisation and commodification of education. The initiatives, ambitions and 'visions' of the companies work on the education system, as a form of economic attrition, converting public into private goods. The actors broker arrangements across the public–private divide, and bring new practices, values and sensibilities into play. They take up roles within the discourse and infrastructure of reform, converting education policy into a different sort of language, invested with different sorts of relationships, interests and purposes.

Pearson Education – global giant!

Here I want to explore the global reach of edu-business, and business growth and acquisitions, and their possible consequences for education policy, a little further, by focusing on Pearson Education, the world's largest education company.

> Pearson Education is part of the global media and education group *Pearson*, and a sister company of *Penguin* and the *Financial Times* newspaper. Every day our books and learning tools help people around the world to grow their knowledge, develop their skills and realise their potential.
>
> With offices in over 30 countries, Pearson Education has built an international reach that enables us to provide the most comprehensive sales, marketing and distribution for the books we publish. We have the expertise to exploit the multiple sales channels and an increasing proportion of our business coming from new formats and markets.
>
> (Pearson website)

As well as the *Financial Times* and Penguin Books, Pearson owns several other publishing houses, Edexcel (the University of London Examination

Board, as was), and 50 per cent of the FTSE index (recently sold for £450 million) and of *The Economist*. Pearson's worldwide sales in 2009 were £5.1bn; in 2010, Group sales increased 10 per cent to £5.7bn, while pre-tax profit rose 28 per cent to £670 million, and the company has 37,000 employees worldwide. In the past three years Pearson has pursed an aggressive global programme of acquisitions and joint ventures, as we shall see. In May 2010 Pearson agreed to sell its stake in financial data provider Interactive Data for $3.4bn 'to free up funds for acquisitions in emerging markets' (Reuters). The Chief Executive of Pearson is Dame Marjorie Scardino, whose 'remuneration package' for 2009–10 was more than £2.3m. When she joined the company in 1997 the share price was £6.66; as I write it stands at £11.74 (12.31 p.m. 15 July 2011).

Pearson generates 21 per cent of its income from US higher education publishing, e.g. MyLab digital learning, homework and assessment programmes, CourseConnect online courses, and the eCollege online management system. A further 21 per cent of income comes from assessment and information work in the US, including running the Florida state schools testing programme, and the Powerschool and Chancery student information systems, and 12 per cent comes from school curriculum sales, e.g. enVisionMATH, and Poptropica, a virtual world for young children. Pearson recently (August 2010) acquired America's Choice (an education and information company, see Chapter 5), 'a leading provider of school improvement services' for $80m cash. In July 2010 it established a strategic partnership with Sistema Educacional Brasileiro (SEB) and acquired SEB's school learning systems (for £326m); this serves 450,000 students in public and private schools in Brazil. Globally, Pearson won new contracts in Colombia (eCollege), South Africa and Malta, Vietnam and the UK (Pearson Learning Solutions) in 2009–10. The UK generates 7 per cent of Pearson's income (it runs BTEC, a vocational qualification and the Edexcel examination board) and in May 2010 Pearson bought Melorio, a UK vocational training company which has 49 training centres, for £99m (Melorio's profit after tax for 2010 was £520,000). In 2008 Melorio had purchased Zenos Learning for £20.6m and Learning World Academies when it was floated on the stock exchange. Europe generates 5 per cent of income via, for example, Linx secondary science in Italy, and the development of a virtual business community in the Netherlands. A further 2 per cent of income comes from Africa and the Middle East, including national contracts in Ethiopia for science learning materials, and a UNICEF contract to provide 13.5m textbooks in Zimbabwe. Another 4 per cent comes from Asia, including a new joint venture with Educomp (see Chapter 4); in 2009 Pearson paid $30m for a 50 per cent stake in Educomp's vocational training businesses, which have 12 million users in 23,000 schools in India, North America and Singapore, and also bought a controlling stake in another Indian company, TutorVista, for $127m, which provides offshore online tutoring for US students (at a fifth of the cost of US-based tutors), and has a network of

60 centres across India delivering tuition courses and a school development service. Latin America contributes 2 per cent of income, with new developments in Brazil, Mexico and Colombia. The professional testing and publishing division produces 6 per cent of sales with new contracts in Saudi Arabia, Egypt, Bahrain and Colorado, US, for testing medical and business professionals.

In November 2010 Pearson acquired US company The Administrative Assistants, a provider of student information systems, for an undisclosed sum. In March 2011 it made a cash offer of £113m for vocational and professional education company Education Development International. EDI is accredited by the UK government to award a wide range of vocational qualifications, including apprenticeships and diplomas. EDI's expertise is in quality-assuring work-based training programmes, working closely with employers and over 1,500 private training providers and further education colleges. Internationally, EDI trades under the London Chamber of Commerce and Industry brand and offers a range of business and English language qualifications. LCCI International Qualifications are widely used in South-East Asia and over 100 countries around the world. In April 2011 Pearson announced the acquisition of Schoolnet, a fast-growing US education technology company, for $230m in cash. Pearson also aims to become 'the world's pre-eminent provider of English language learning content, technology and services' (Pearson wesbite) and in September 2010 Pearson acquired the Wall Street Institute chain of language schools for $92m. WSI, which had revenues of $60m in 2009, uses a proprietary learning method and has over 400 franchised language schools in 27 countries, including 40 in China. Pearson intends to invest to expand the chain in growth areas (see Rizvi & Lingard, 2010, pp. 176–79 for a discussion of the global spread of English language learning). Pearson has also expanded its operations in China, Nigeria and South Africa. In 2011 Pearson signed a new Memorandum of Understanding with the Chinese Ministry of Education and the General Administration of Press and Publishing, to cover a range of activities, including: supporting teacher training in China; expanding and strengthening the pool of translators; working to strengthen digital rights management; working collaboratively on language learning and assessment in both Chinese and English. Alongside its business activities Pearson is also involved in educational philanthropy through the work of the Pearson Foundation.

Increasingly edu-businesses like Pearson, in their advertising and promotion, position themselves as offering 'solutions' to the national policy problems of raising standards and achieving educational improvements linked to both individual opportunity and national competitiveness. Such promotion also extends to active participation in policy influence relationships and policy networks (as in the agreement with China) as a means to agitate for policies which offer further opportunities for profit (see Burch, 2009 for examples of edu-business lobbying in the USA in relation to the

No Child Left Behind programme). Indeed Pearson organises development events which are aimed at attracting key policy actors.

Pearson International Education Conference Launched in Singapore
The Pearson Foundation hosted the first annual Pearson International Education Conference April 28–May 1, 2008, in Singapore. The summit, created in partnership with the Council of Chief State School Officers (CCSSO), convened delegates from around the world to share and consider key educational, assessment, and professional development practices that ensure student success in mathematics and science education.

Delegates from countries including Brazil, Canada, England, Italy, Japan, Korea, New Zealand, South Africa, Taiwan, the United Kingdom, and the United States met in small working teams to present and share best practices from their countries; learn from each other ways in which they can improve their own local efforts; and make recommendations that can be shared with an even broader group about methods, practice, and policy in math and science education.

(Pearson website)

In July 2011 Pearson announced the appointment of Sir Michael Barber as their Chief Education Advisor (see Chapter 5). The announcement said that 'he will lead Pearson's world wide programme of research into education policy and efficacy, advise on and support the development of products and services that build on the research findings, and play a particular role in Pearson's strategy for education in the poorest parts of the world...' (company website). Barber himself is quoted as saying: 'The opportunity for governments and businesses to transform learning outcomes for people of all ages has never been greater – and the need to do so never more urgent'. Here again, in both extracts, within a business strategy, we see business growth articulated in relation to the taking up of a moral position, and a position in relation to education policy and 'policywork'.

All of this has a variety of consequences in terms of national education policies and policy influence and transnational standardisation, and processes of Westernisation, as well as signalling further aspects of the wholesale commodification of education and educational processes. Pearson is a globalising actor in a very real sense, through its publishing, its assessment and qualifications systems, English language teaching and administration and management products. It is operating across all three educational 'message systems' – pedagogy, curriculum and assessment and joining these up, globally, across a range of media, within its products and business growth plan. Its publishing and curriculum and assessment work contributes to define what cultural knowledge is most worthwhile and these products have invested within them particular conceptions of educational process and organisation. Pearson is increasingly interested in the work of 'improving' schools. It is active in defining problems and solving them. Its clients are both private and public sector learners, organisations and governments. By virtue of its reach and size Pearson is able to deal directly with national governments and multilateral agencies – as in the instances of China and UNICEF – and it can provide 'one-off' solutions to national and international development problems. Pearson is a serious policy player, a key part of 'the new global geometry of power' (Rizvi & Lingard, 2010, p. 172) in education, but nonetheless, for the most part, goes unnoticed in education policy analysis.

Selling students

It is not only educational materials and services and policy ideas that are being sold by the edu-businesses. There is now a global market in educational institutions – schools, colleges and universities (and in effect their clients – students) are bought and sold (as in the cases of John Bauer and AcadeMedia above).

In particular, there is a set of global brands which are emerging and are increasingly dominant in the lucrative private higher education market. One such is Laureate Education, a US-based private higher education company which owns 51 universities around the world and which had an income of US$160 million in 2005. Laureate is owned by the private equity company KKR – Kohlberg, Kravis, Roberts and Co (www.kkr.com/).

> Laureate Education, Inc. is dedicated to helping its students reach their highest potential and supporting their achievement of personal and professional goals. Laureate brings to its universities and students a global perspective blended with a local point of view, creating a truly multicultural, career-oriented educational experience.
>
> (http://www.ordinate.com/share/leu/LaureatePilotReport.pdf, accessed 10 July 2011)

For example, included in their global portfolio of universities are two in Brazil; Universidade Anhembi Morumbi (UAM, Brazil) founded in 1970 as a school of tourism and Faculdade Unida da Paraiba (UniPB, Brazil), founded in 2006. UniPB serves more than 550 students, offering degrees in nutrition, nursing, environmental engineering and gastronomy.

This is a particular sort of knowledge economy; the monetary value and profitability of education here are very self-evident and most direct. Again there are both opportunities and dangers involved for national governments. These institutional forms of higher education may provide quick and relatively cheap means to up-skill the local workforce in response to the supposed requirements of the global knowledge economy, as well as satisfying the increased local demand for access to HE, especially those which offer forms of certification with international currency and thus potential entry into the global labour market. In India, Brazil and China in particular a significant expansion in private higher education has been a response to local political and economic pressures. The gross enrolment rate in HE in China has risen from 6 per cent to 23 per cent in the past decade (Choudaha, 2001), but graduate unemployment is rising fast and 'the supply of higher education has increased at great pace but without an emphasis on quality' (p. 27). China has allowed the entry of foreign providers as a response to demand and skills needs, and around 500 foreign campuses are up and running in China, although the government has now suspended further recognition of overseas providers. Other states, like Singapore, have encouraged 'elite' overseas providers to set up shop as a means of attracting overseas students from other parts of South-East Asia and beyond, and in an effort to reinvent itself as a 'global classroom' and a regional hub for HE. By 2003 there were 14 elite transnational campuses in Singapore, including MIT, INSEAD (France), University of Chicago and IIT (India). In some cases these are notionally 'public' universities acting in a private, for-profit capacity. These offshore enterprises may also be seen as part of a new educational colonialism. Business schools in particular have been key points for the articulation and flow of new, Western, and particularly US, management ideas and metaphors. There are also, as noted, difficult issues about quality and accountability involved. In many cases these private university chains employ poorly qualified teachers and have a limited involvement in research activities (McCowan, 2004). Indeed companies like Pearson can offer HE companies software packages which provide curriculum materials, learning systems, and online assessment and marking, together with administrative systems, which require only minimal design and teaching inputs.

Let us look a little more closely at the financial and network complexity embedded in these sorts of international HE developments, and some further aspects of blurring between traditional public/private sector divisions (see Figure 6.1).

Exporting excellence

In 2000 the University of Nottingham opened a campus in Malaysia (UNiM). UNiM has 2,700 students from 50 different countries and Nottingham's UK, Malaysia and Chinese campuses (see below) now enrol over 30,000 students. The majority shareholder of UNiM is the Boustead Group, an engineering services and geospatial technology company. Nottingham spent £5.3 million on the Malaysia campus, and it owns a 29.1 per cent share (*Times Higher Education* 27 September 2007). It is not clear how Nottingham funded its investment in UNiM. The third partner is YTL Corporation Berhad, which owns and manages utilities and 'infrastructural assets' and owns 19 per cent of UNiM. This is perhaps an example of what Kelsey (2006) suggests is 'an unsustainable hybrid

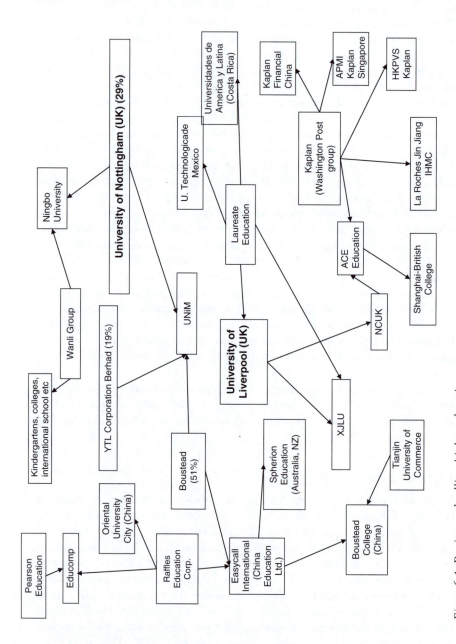

Figure 6.1 Buying and selling higher education.

form of a modern/neoliberal university' (p. 1). UNiM awards University of Nottingham degrees. In effect, perhaps, Nottingham is licensing its trademark but the vice-chancellor at the time, Sir Colin Campbell, was adamant that a 'Franchise arrangement is too great a risk to reputation' and that 'Exams, marking and quality assurance are consistent' (*EducationGuardian*, 4 September 2007). The university describe their overseas strategy as 'exporting excellence' (Annual Report 2005). The University of Nottingham won the Queen's Award for Enterprise in 2006 and 2007. Furthermore, Newcastle and Southampton universities currently have campuses under construction in Malaysia's 'Educity' in Johor and Australia's Monash University already operates in Malaysia, as does MIT. The Netherlands Maritime Institute of Technology is already in Educity and Johns Hopkins is planning a medical school there.

UNiM was not the Boustead Group's only educational investment. An associate company of the Boustead group, Easycall International (China Education Ltd.) owned Boustead College in China, a joint enterprise with Tianjin University of Commerce. In 2004 Easycall purchased Spherion Education, a New Zealand company that runs 13 training institutes in Australia and New Zealand. Easycall has since been bought by the Raffles Education Corp., a Singapore-based company which owns Oriental University City (China) and which has grown from its founding in 1990 to operate three universities and 26 colleges across 10 countries in the Asia-Pacific region.

Nottingham university also has strong market relations with China and the number of Chinese students at Nottingham in the UK is well over 1,000. Nottingham is also involved in a joint-venture university in China. Nottingham owns a 37.5 per cent share in the Ningbo University campus, a joint venture with the state-owned Wanli Education Group. The Wanli Education Group is an independent provider that runs a full range of educational services, from kindergartens to the Chinese equivalent of a university college. Since its establishment in 1993 the Wanli Education Group has invested nearly $US 60m and the group is responsible for nine institutions, including an international school, a vocational college and a night school. The creation of opportunities for Chinese students to study abroad and the provision of wider access at home are key elements of the group's strategy. Wanli provided the infrastructure for Ningbo, worth £14 million. Douglas Tallack, professor of American studies and pro-vice-chancellor of Nottingham, explained that about 30 per cent of the 'total investment' has come from Nottingham and that that figure includes notional values given to contributions in the form of non-monetary intellectual property rights. In terms of hard cash, the university has made a 'modest investment' it has been said. Some of the university library stock has been moved to the China campus. The licence to operate the University of Nottingham-Ningbo is valid until 2055 (Ministry of Education, 5 September 2007).

Nottingham University: reaping 'A Phenomenal return on a £40 million investment'

21 September 2007 Nottingham University's Ningbo campus now has 2,850 students studying for degrees equivalent to those in the UK. Nottingham says its aim is to build research and industry links with China and to improve student mobility between the countries.

(www.timeshighereducation.co.uk/story.asp?story-Code=310522&sectioncode=26. accessed 1 July 2009)

In 2007, Liverpool University also launched a joint-venture university in China – the Xi'an Jiaotong Liverpool University near Shanghai. Liverpool has a 30 per cent stake in this joint venture but the financial backing for Liverpool's stake comes from Laureate Education (see above). The company also provided the £1million bond necessary for the University of Liverpool to operate in China. XJLU is a free-standing institution, which awards its own degrees and 'The purpose of this ambitious project was to boost Liverpool's global brand' according to the HE think tank Agora (Fazackerley, 2007, p. 26). The University of Liverpool is not directly responsible for quality or standards. The university is run by a board, whose members include the US company Laureate, the Suzhou Industrial Park and the Chinese partner university. Laureate also owns and runs the Les Roches Jin Jiang International Hotel Management College and Sichuan Tianyi University in China. XJLU is listed on their website as one of their universities.

Laureate also provides the platform for Liverpool's online degrees (this was begun as a partnership with the Dutch corporation K.I.Telearning in 1999; Laureate bought K.I.T. in 2004) and in 2007 Liverpool announced another agreement with Laureate which will allow Laureate students to study on Liverpool summer school programmes, established dual degrees with students taking parts of their degree in each university system, and joint curriculum design projects in health sciences, information technology and the humanities. Liverpool may also set up onsite courses at Laureate Campuses. In 2006 Laureate took over the technology, student and human resources and financial management services of Bilgi University, Turkey, in a partnership arrangement.

Liverpool is also involved in a number of projects with Kaplan. Kaplan is a subsidiary of the Washington Post Company (owned by News International) and has 70 HE campuses in the US in 20 states (as well as a variety of other HE services) and campuses also in China, Hong Kong and Singapore. In 2007 Kaplan's revenue was in excess of $2bn. In 1987 11 UK universities banded together to form NCUK (Northern Consortium United Kingdom – there are now 22 partners including 5 Irish universities), which provides overseas transition centres for students wanting to study in the UK (including in China, Ireland, Japan, Kenya, Nigeria, South Korea, Sri Lanka, United Arab Emirates, The United Kingdom and Vietnam). The local partner in China is ACE Education and in 2006 NCUK and ACE opened the Shanghai-British College. In April 2007 Kaplan took a minority interest in ACE and in November 2007 became the majority owner of Kaplan ACE. Liverpool and Kaplan have also established an international college located on the campus of the University of Liverpool. The aim is to prepare international students for entry into the university's undergraduate and graduate degree programmes. Such colleges are already in existence in partnership with the University of Sheffield, the University of Glasgow and Nottingham Trent University.

Clearly, within these relationships, roles and exchanges, what may have been a clear demarcation between public and private higher education, between public service and profit, is now thoroughly blurred. The financial activities of 'public sector' universities are complexly intertwined with those of the private sector. While Marginson (2006) argues that in the higher echelons of global HE it is status rather than profitability that is being competed for, the two often go hand in hand, especially as the fallout from the global financial crises reduces funding of and recruitment to public HE from traditional sources.

> Research-intensive universities like Melbourne, Sydney, New South Wales and Queensland have been forced to exhibit a Jekyll and Hyde personality in the global environment. At home they are selective and focused on research and they engage in global benchmarking and cross-border research collaborations. But they also have another international agenda, identical to that of the 32 lesser Australia universities, which is to build a massive fee-paying enrolment to fill the revenue gap.
>
> (Marginson, 2006, p. 26)

In addition to the examples quoted above, the Harvard Business School now has a branch in Delhi, and Columbia University has announced the opening of a number of global research centres (Paris, Mumbai, Beijing and Amman). Again we need to consider whether these actors (the organisations and their employees) are doing 'globalising' and doing 'neoliberalising' work. Marginson (2006, p. 1) also makes the point that: 'there can be no global flows of people, money, messages, ideas and policies without globalizing and globalized human agents (Marginson & Sawir, 2005). Globalization is inside higher education as well as outside. We are all implicated in it (though some have more moving power than others)'. The funding of public sector HE is increasingly opaque and the moral and educational bases of educational practices are increasingly murky. Viewed in terms of the developments outlined above, Western public universities are now 'hybrid organisational forms in which public and private interests are combined' (Clarke & Newman, 1997). Kelsey (2006) argues that 'University/business collaborations deepen the influence of corporate priorities and preferences and compress critical space' (p. 9). Nottingham and Liverpool, and many others, are no longer in any straightforward sense national public universities, they are transnational, corporate and profit-oriented, and they are positioned on the boundaries between academia and business – they are hybrids. More generally Thrift (2005, p. 23) argues that there are 'an increasing number of symmetries between academia and business'. These universities are involved in complex 'border-crossing' relationships with the private sector, state agencies, international consortia and other national states. Partnerships, linkages and networks 'join up' state organisations with commercial ones and create discursive capillaries through which the sensibilities and dispositions of enterprise flow and the ontology of neo-liberalism is generalised. Complex relationships built upon contract rather than collegiality and aimed at profit generation rather than knowledge production or public service enfold public universities into the field of commerce.

Alongside the universities there are now a variety of schools operating internationally. There are the global chains, as noted previously, run by companies like NordAnglia, GEMS and John Bauer and a small number of export brands like England's Marlborough College, which is building a 900-student campus in Malaysia's Educity, and Dulwich College, which has campuses in China and Korea.

> Dulwich College Management International (DCMI) commenced operations in China, with the establishment of Dulwich College in Shanghai, a co-educational, non-denominational academic institution offering education to the expatriate community, based on the same educational philosophy of Dulwich College London. Following the success of the Shanghai College DCMI have established Dulwich College in Beijing, Suzhou, and Zhuhai in China as well as in Seoul, Korea.
>
> (http://www.dulwichcollege.cn/)

Some of these schools are aimed at the increasingly large, mobile, global middle class (see Ball, 2010a), while others recruit local students whose parents are seeking high-status English language education and qualifications for their children. Furthermore, working with a different direction of flow, the national public schools systems in countries like Canada, New Zealand and Australia are marketed by their governments to recruit fee-paying, overseas school students, from as young as five. As Martens and Starke (2008, p. 15) report, in the case of New Zealand: 'The spectacular growth of its export education industry – as indicated by student numbers and estimates of foreign currency earnings – has been accompanied by domestic and international government policies facilitating this trend'. This is what Martens and Starke call 'trade driven policy in education' (p. 15), and countries like New Zealand (the 'Contact Group'), have been in the forefront of moves within the World Trade Organisation to facilitate the international deregulation of educational services. Here again, in a different way, neo-liberal states play a key role in the development of global education markets in sponsoring and marketing their educational 'exporters' – public and private – and in the work of what Jessop (2002, p. 240) calls 'metaexchange', in their home systems, that is 'the reflexive design of individual markets (for example, for land, labour, money, commoditions, knowledge – or appropriate subdivisions thereof) and/or the reflexive reordering of relations among markets by modifying their operation and articulation' (pp. 240–41).

Discussion

So we have come full circle, from business and the market, back to the state and have identified a set of complex relationships and actual or latent tensions. There are both opportunities and dangers here for the 'competition state' – conflicts and mutual-dependencies. On the one hand, neo-liberal states are market makers, facilitators of global education business or eager recipients of private participation as they seek to solve problems related to the funding and provision of education for their populations, as in China and Malaysia, or achieve their Millennium Development Goals, as in sub-Saharan Africa, or seek niche positions in the global education market, as in the UK, Australia and New Zealand, and increasingly India.

On the other hand, national and company ambitions are not always compatible and Mok (2007), following Fukuyama, also draws attention to the important differences between states in the scope of their governing and their capacity to govern. Buyouts, consolidations and mergers which involve change of ownership and of scale, as well as market failures, political changes and financial cycles, will all have their effects on the influence, capabilities and ambitions of global edu-businesses, and national boundaries are only of relative significance here, as 'capital continually renders obsolete the very geographical landscapes it creates and upon which its own reproduction and expansion hinges' (Brenner & Theodore, 2002, p. 354). There is no simple local–global dualism that can be evoked here, rather a set of evolving 'connections' which cut across scales and territories and sectors. Governments, international agencies and institutions and businesses struggle over the development and control of these (see Yang, Vidovich & Currie, 2007). These struggles cut across academic, financial and political agendas and interests and they are increasingly dynamic. Global edu-business is fast-developing and fast-changing, eager to open up new spaces for expansion – to commodify more and more of the social – while concomitantly post-crisis, cash-strapped states everywhere construct 'leaner' bureaucracies, implement financial austerity programmes while seeking new ways to up-skill and flexibilise their human capital.

Notes

1 In the 2010 UK election campaign the Conservative Party manifesto indicated that a Conservative government would introduce Swedish-style Free Schools.

2 John Chubb is on the Board of Directors of Education Sector; he is the CEO of Leeds Global Partners, LLC. Previously Chubb was founder, senior executive vice president for new product development, and managing director of The Edison Learning Institute. Before joining Edison in 1992, Chubb was a senior fellow at The Brookings Institution and a professor at Stanford University. Chubb currently is a distinguished visiting fellow at the Hoover Institution at Stanford University.

3 Advantage Schools is a Boston-based company that runs eight charter schools in seven states. Education is conducted in a formal environment in which students wear uniforms and 'zero-tolerance' for disruptive behaviour is enforced. Each school maintains a 'Code of Civility' by which all students are expected to abide. The growth of Advantage was supported by a $10m investment by several venture capital firms, led by Kleiner Perkins Caufield & Byers of Menlo Park, CA. Also investing were Bessemer Venture Partners of Wellesley, Fidelity Ventures of Boston and United States Trust Co. of New York.

4 Pioneer Institute is an independent, non-partisan, privately funded research organisation that seeks to improve the quality of life in Massachusetts through civic discourse and intellectually rigorous, data-driven public policy solutions based on free-market principles, individual liberty and responsibility, and the ideal of effective, limited and accountable government.

5 A City Technology College (CTC) is a state-funded all-ability secondary school that charges no fees but is independent of local authority control, being overseen directly by the Department for Education. One fifth of the capital costs are met by private business sponsors, who also own or lease the buildings. The CTC programme was established in the late 1980s by the Conservative government under the terms of the Education Reform Act 1988 and the colleges themselves opened in the late 1980s and early 1990s.

7 Money, meaning and policy connections

> There is a growing sense that social policies are taking new directions as policy debates move from an earlier embrace of privatization and marketization, to the task of retooling the state to face new social risks and to reproduce the social (social cohesion, social capital, social inclusion, social economy). Nevertheless, some have argued that these are shifts within a broader and uneven process of neo-liberalization and represent the rolling-out of new institutions and governmentalities to stabilize neo-liberal accumulation strategies. This position nevertheless conceals disagreement between a view of new policies 'flanking' neo-liberalism through the marginal introduction of non-market logics, and those rolling out market metrics into further realms of social life.
>
> This nevertheless poses the issue at a high level of abstraction, and risks positing a logic divorced from the messy realm of policy development. It can ultimately be criticized for underplaying the degree of diversity within neoliberalism, as well as for ignoring bottom-up influences on policy. There is thus a need to track patterns of neoliberal restructuring and make part–whole connections between local instances of policy reform and broader neoliberal discourses.
>
> (Graefe, 2005, p. 2)

In a number of ways Graefe's summary of neo-liberal analysis here touches on the main concerns of this book – the identification of a new generation of global education policies; the need to think about the ambitions and limits to neo-liberalism, at the same time; and the changing forms and modalities of the state in relation to 'the neo-liberal'; the breaking down of the boundaries between the social and the economic, and the political and the economic; the messiness and mix of policy rationalities and forms of regulation and governance currently in play; and crucially, the need to track and examine examples of 'actually existing' neo-liberal restructuring and its geographical polyvalency. I have been trying here to map some of the 'emergent geographies of neoliberalisation' (Peck & Tickell, 2003, p. 22). We need to think about neo-liberalism within and beyond nation states, as a set of practices, as well as doctrines, and as a process, uneven and sometimes 'slow and clumsy' (Rinne, Kivirauma & Simola, 2002, p. 655), and as sometimes subject to blockage and opposition – as in Finland (see Rinne et al., 2002) or as recently in Chile (see Cole, 2012; Jones, 2010). We must be wary of crude totalizing accounts, and of simple elisions of neo-liberalism and globalization, indeed the 'under-specified processes of globalization are often inappropriately ascribed a kind of omnipresent causal efficacy' (Peck & Tickell, 2003, p. 20).

I have sought to address this agenda by getting down to cases, by looking at the ways in which policy is being reconceived and reconstituted in the shift from bureaucracy and hierarchy to networks and heterarchy. *There is* a proliferation of policy networks nationally and globally made up of 'operationally autonomous' but 'structurally coupled' organisations (Jessop, 2002, p. 202). New policy networks and communities are being established through which neo-liberal discourses and knowledge flow and gain legitimacy and credibility. These are new policy assemblages with a diverse range of old and new participants existing in a new kind of policy space somewhere between multilateral agencies, national governments and international business, in and beyond the traditional sites and circulations of policymaking. I have argued that this shift is bringing into play a new form of governance, albeit not in a single and coherent form, and concomitantly bringing new sources of authority into the policy process (globally and nationally) and indeed establishing a 'market of authorities' (Shamir, 2008, p. 10); there are new voices within policy conversations and new conduits through which policy discourses enter policy thinking. The moral and financial 'authority' and capitals of corporate philanthropy is one major new voice which needs careful attention (see Kovacs, 2010; Saltman, 2010). Within all of this the modalities and contents of education policy and service delivery are changing nationally and internationally in many different settings as edu-business seeks new profit opportunities, and the educational state is increasingly congested and increasingly opaque and there is a new mix within the matrix of governance involving increasingly 'complex relations of reciprocal interdependence' (Jessop, 2002, p. 52). The boundaries between state, economy and civil society are being reworked, as languages, practices and values converge and actors and discourse move. As a result there is also for national governments, in some respects, especially those of small and fragile states, a reduction in their capacity to steer their education systems. At the same time there is a duality of deconcentration and centralization – more relative autonomy for public sector service organisations (of diverse kinds) but new mechanisms and techniques of central steering. That is, the development and insinuation of new 'arts of government' enacted in new policy technologies. In these new processes of policy, states are changing, being changed and to some extent being residualised, or as Hannam, Sheller and Urry (2006, p. 2) put it, 'the nation itself is being transformed by [such] mobilities'.

It is tempting and somehow trite, but nonetheless true, to say that this is a complex, unstable and difficult terrain of research. In many respects we have neither the language and concepts nor the methods and techniques appropriate for researching neo-liberal practices. These developments and changes in education policy, affecting the forms and modalities of educational provision and organisation, have outrun the current purview of our research agenda and we need to adapt and adjust what it is we consider as research problems in order to catch up. We need to ask different questions and also to look in different places for answers to these questions. We may also need some new skills and sensibilities if we are going to address them sensibly. In particular we must begin to draw upon forms of business and financial analysis, or to put it another way, we must 'follow the money'. That is, among other things, policy researchers have to become regular readers of the *Financial Times* and *Wall Street Journal*, and stock market reports, and must learn to read company accounts.

Show me the money!

The unstated and usually unexamined subtext of neo-liberalism is not doctrine but money, particularly and crucially in the form of profit. Of course states are also about money. Policies cost money, and that money must come from somewhere, and one of the responses of states around the world to the 2008 financial crisis has been to make 'cuts' in public spending and to look for ways of doing policy cheaper – marketization and privatization are taken to be one way of doing policy cheaper, as well as more effectively. 'The expansion of market relations allows, in theory, a lower level of public spending, and therefore a lower level of taxation' (Connell, Fawcett & Meagher, 2009, p. 332). However, in most education policy research money is rarely mentioned and is overwritten by a focus on ideas and practices. Even when subjected to the arcane mercies of the economics of education, issues of funding are dealt with as abstractions. However, in the interface between education policy and neo-liberalism, money is everywhere. As I have indicated, policy itself is now bought and sold, it is a commodity and a profit opportunity, there is a growing global market in policy ideas. Policy work is also increasingly being outsourced to profit-making organisations, who bring their skills, discourses and sensibilities to the policy table, for an hourly rate or on contract to the state.

Alongside this, bits of policy, bits of the state, bits of statework, are now owned by the private sector – these bits are also traded. Private equity and global education businesses are interested in profitable education enterprises. State schools and hospitals, built through PFI and PPP schemes, are owned and run by banks, builders and management service companies and leased back to the state – and are again often very profitable and again are traded. I also touched upon the market in private educational organisations – schools and universities – which are being bought and sold, bundled together, merged. In all of this education is a service commodity, or is real estate (buildings and infrastructure), or a brand, alongside any other commodity or capital asset, and is treated accordingly, subject to the same business strategies, the same generic management techniques, and the same systems of value (in both senses of the word). This of course brings into play new kinds of decision-making, new 'bottom-lines', new interests. In the world of business shareholders, investors and stock market value – profitability is what counts in the final analysis.

Nonetheless, the argument is now being made that the disciplines of profit are what is needed to reform and re-energise the public sector; either in the form of 'social capitalism' or 'social enterprise'. That is, enterprise can succeed where the state has failed. As Bill Gates argued at the 2008 World Economic Forum:

> The Challenge here is to design a system where market incentives, including profits and recognition, drive those principles to do more for the poor.
> I like to call this idea creative capitalism, an approach where governments, businesses, and nonprofits work together to stretch the reach of market forces so that more people can make a profit, or gain recognition, doing work that eases the world's inequities.
> (http://www.microsoft.com/presspass/exec/billg/speeches/
> 2008/01-24wefdavos.mspx)

Here then profit becomes a force for good, at exactly the same time as it brought the Western financial system to the brink of collapse.

The discipline of profit, through enterprise and entrepreneurism, is being used to neo-liberalize public sector education from within and without – endogenously and exogenously. In the former, by devolving budgets and encouraging educational institutions to be entrepreneurial, and thus to generate increasing amounts of their budget from non-state sources, as well as to seek ways of cutting their costs. This is interrelated with, and partly dependent upon, policies of labour force deregulation and flexibilitization, and tends to produce 'a growing workforce of part-time and casual contract labour at the bottom of organisations' (Connell et al., 2009, p. 332) – the deployment of learning support assistants in English schools is a case in point.

As I suggested in Chapter 6, the critical point of interface between market and state is that of regulation, as represented in neo-liberal discourse in the concept of 'limited government'. Increasingly within contemporary politics the issue is not whether there should be public service markets or not – market logics have become 'naturalised' (Peck & Tickell, 2003, p. 17) – but how much and how loosely/tightly regulated. The state is increasingly involved in facilitating, extending and managing markets. This includes replacing state organisations with voluntary, social-purpose or profit organisations, through the contracting out of services or by making more private education provision available both in the form of private universities, high-cost international schools, private school chains, low-cost, storefront schools for the poor, and various forms of virtual and online learning.

Money, as profit, is significant, and, I have argued, needs to be researched in another sense. I have given particular emphasis in this account to the role of philanthropy as well as business, and particularly to business philanthropy, in global education policy. The 'new' philanthropists like Gates, Omidyar, Dell, Walton, Broad and so on want to 'give back' that which they generated in the form of profit from their businesses. However, they want to use their donations in a businesslike way, as 'investments' with good returns. Here money is power in a number of ways. The power to get things done – build schools, start up programmes, pay for bursaries – the power to 'partner' with governments in solving social problems, and the power to speak and enact policy, sometimes over and against the wishes of governments, in local and transnational arenas. As a result, to reiterate, policy is being done in different places now – there is a respatialization of policy. Indeed, new policy initiatives, like low-cost schools for the poor, attract financial 'investment' from both business and business philanthropy – venture capital and venture philanthropists – and are producing new sorts of organisations and organisational relationships that blur traditional distinctions between public, voluntary, philanthropic and for-profit. There are then, perhaps, different sorts of money involved here. There is big money and small money; both multinational businesses and local entrepreneurs; multi-million dollar investments and microloans. The microfinance business is enterprise as a solution to social and economic problems writ small (Stewart, van Rooyen, Dickson, Majoro & de Wet, 2011). In India, microfinance is now indeed a business, and some multinational banks are also getting interested in generating profit through such microloans. This is moving a long way from the original principles of Muhammad Yunus and the Grameen Bank. More research is needed on the evolving microfinance sector, although a recent systematic review of microcredit research concluded that:

> ... some people are made poorer, and not richer, by microfinance, particularly micro-credit clients. This seems to be because: they consume more instead of investing in their futures; their businesses fail to produce enough profit to pay high interest rates; their investment in other longer-term aspects of their futures is not sufficient to give a return on their investment; and because the context in which microfinance clients live is by definition fragile.
>
> (Stewart et al., 2011, p. 6)

Money is also important in getting neo-liberalism, as a doctrine and as a set of policy ideas, into the public and political imagination. That is, funding for advocacy, 'research' and 'influence' activities in making neo-liberalism thinkable, possible, obvious and necessary as 'a new dominant social ideology' (Connell et al., 2009, p. 333). This is part of what Peck and Tickell refer to as the 'deep process' of neo-liberalisation, and they argue that 'one of the more far-reaching effects of this deep process of neo-liberalisation has been the attempt to sequester key economic policy issues beyond the reach of explicit politicisation' (Peck & Tickell, 2003, p. 16). This is done, in part, within various forms of policy advocacy, and I have tried to account for some of the very organised ways in which, again, money and ideas work to join up advocacy activities to policy proposals and to programmes of reform. This is another form of the investment of profits for future returns. In this case capital, through philanthropic foundations, invests in the work of think tanks and advocacy networks and policy entre-preneurs with the intention and hope of exacting extensions to the commo-dification of the social, the creation of new markets and the deregulation of existing ones. As Connell et al. (2009, p. 333) put it: 'Neoliberals continue to attack public enterprise, bureaucrats, red tape, regulatory agencies, unions, cooperatives, welfare dependency, and other hangovers from what they see as a discredited past'. In relation to this, neo-liberalism is well organised and very practical. Networks like Atlas, IPN, Stockholm and Mont Pelerin enable the movement of ideas, the legitimatization of policy, the bringing of influence to bear, the process of attrition in relation to the 'discredited past' as a 'sociocultural logic' (Connell, Fawcett et al., 2009, p. 333). All of this goes some way towards demonstrating that neo-liberalism is neither natural nor inevitable (Peck & Tickell, 2003); it is being done and planned and enacted.

One of the frustrations and failings of the analysis attempted in this book has been the analytic, practical, aesthetic and representational difficulties involved in conceptualising and communicating the extent, density and multifacetedness of the connectivity, the 'entanglements', which embeds, enables and enacts this process of transformation. Through examples I have sought to demonstrate and examine the intimate but often unapparent relationships between critique, advocacy, philanthropy, social enterprise, business (of various kinds), academia and politics. I have also highlighted the role of key individuals in joining up these social and economic fields – as carriers of the discourse and practice of neo-liberalism. This connectivity is the tissue, the substance of neo-liberal attrition and advance – roll-back and roll-out. It is evident in links between US charter schools, private equity companies, venture philanthropies, organisations critical of public education, think tanks, and freelance educational consultants. It is evident in links between pro-market foundations, policy entrepreneurs, government depart-ments, the World Bank, NGOs and commercial reading schemes. It is evident in links between the funding of educational conferences, the pub-lication of pro-market research and edu-businesses. It is evident in relations between multinational banks, their Foundations, not-for-profit educational providers in late-developing countries and new business opportunities. It is evident in a new generation of hybrid policy entrepreneurs who operate across advocacy, politics, philanthropy and business – whom Dezalay and Garth (2002, p. 30) call neo-liberal *technopols* and who are 'strongly embedded in an international market of expertise modeled on the United States' and who Peck identifies as the 'principal agents' of roll-out neo-liberalism. These *technopols* play a key role in what Dezalay and Garth (2002) call the 'dollarization' of post-Keynesian statecraft, which takes place through a set of complex, dense and intersecting networks which link together business schools, economic courses, treasuries and finance ministries, policy agencies, think tanks and multilateral agencies. I have focused considerable attention on James Tooley as one such technopol and policy entrepreneur, partly because his activities focus specifically on education and education policy, partly because he is prominent, indeed ubiquitous, in the global education policy field, and partly because his modus operandi exemplifies the work of policy mobility and roll-out neo-liberalism. He operates on a number of levels, to give legitimacy to neo-liberal solutions through research, to persuade and co-opt governments and philanthropists, to construct and animate infrastructures of financial and discursive relations, and to put ideas into practice through start-up enterprises.

Mobilities

Another issue of which this study has made me very aware is the need for methods and sensibilities which are attuned to movement and flow rather than structure and place; that is, we have to avoid or move beyond 'flat' and 'fixed' ontologies. We need to think about 'the temporality of processes, and the dynamic character of the interrelationships between heterogeneous phenomena' (Rizvi & Lingard, 2011, p. 7) as well as 'the dynamics of change in the global era, affected by combinations of material shifts produced by new technologies and mobilities, as well as non-material elements such as globally convergent discourses and locally resisting traditions' (p. 8). This is what Urry (2003, p. 157) calls the 'mobility turn' and Beck (2006) calls a 'cosmopolitan sociology' with a focus on the interconnected, the reciprocal, the nonlinear and dialectical and the mutable and fragile. That is, a focus on the 'spatialising' of social relations, on travel and other forms of movement and other transnational interactions, moments, sites, events and forms of sociality, in relation to policy and 'policywork'. In this account *the network* has provided an analytic trope which is one response to the need for new ways of conceiving of and researching global policy mobilities, alongside more specific attention to events, exchanges, presentations and communication media, social relationships and advocacy. The network refocuses attention on the 'circulatory systems that connect and interpenetrate' the local (Peck, 2003, p. 229). As Urry (2003, p. 170) puts it very simply: 'Social life at least for many in the "west" and "north" is increasingly networked'. However, the network both represents and distorts policy mobilities; it is useful but flawed. It can convey a sense of heterogeneity, connectivity and epistemic community, but also inevitably fixes flows, flattens asymmetries, and lags behind the dynamics of exchange. Networks have a particular and rather dull aesthetic, or rather perhaps they suffer from what Riles (2000, p. 19) calls an 'aesthetic failure'; she sees this as endemic to the network form. Network evolution is particularly important but extremely difficult to capture and to represent. The network as a representation and as a visualisation is also always partial; a great deal of the social in social networks is inaccessible – although Twitter, Facebook and blogs provide new peepholes into the social under-life of policy networks. The aesthetic of the network fails to convey the activities of *networking* which animate and energise social relations. Marcus and Saka (2006) make the same point, but also an opposite point, about assemblage, which is a closely related and more theoretically loaded analytic device.[1] They suggest that assemblage seems 'structural' and 'material and stable' but 'the intent in its aesthetic uses is precisely to undermine such ideas of structure' (p. 102). However, I have tried to give attention both to the organisation and structure of networks, and the transactions that enact and animate them (see Ball & Junemann, 2012 for a fuller discussion of policy network analysis). 'The integration of theory and method is, then, central to this research agenda' (McCann, 2011, p. 41). There is a need for network ethnographies, and case studies of events and conferences – the sites of global education policy. McCann notes that 'there is remarkably little scholarship on how conferences might be studied ethnographically as research sites, where dispersed communities of policy actors come together' (p. 43). The point is that networks are 'relational processes which when realised empirically within distinct time- and space-specific contexts, produce observable results …' (Dicken et al., 2001, p. 91). This is also Peck's argument:

> … the closest one can get to understanding the nature of neoliberalism is to follow its movements, and to triangulate between its ideological, ideational, and institutional currents, between philosophy, politics, and practice. This is necessarily an exercise, moreover, in historical geography, as any such effort must be attentive to the spaces in and through which the neoliberal project has been (re)constructed.
>
> (Peck, 2010, p. 8)

Neo-liberal people

I want to reiterate the point made earlier that neo-liberalism is 'in here' as well as 'out there'. That is, neo-liberalism is economic (a rearrangement of relations between capital and the state) and cultural (new values and sensibilities and relationships) and political (a form of governing, new subjectivities) and is 'extending – at least in potential through every arena of social life' (Connell, Fawcett et al., 2009, p. 333). In particular, and in a sense paradoxically, neo-liberalism works for and against the state in mutually constitutive ways. It destroys some possibilities for older ways of governing and creates new possibilities for new ways of governing, particularly, as indicated in the previous two chapters, through the means of enterprise and responsibility. This works by neo-liberalising us, by making us enterprising and responsible, by offering us the opportunity to succeed, and by making us guilty if we do not – by making us into neo-liberal subjects enmeshed in the 'powers of freedom'. This happens not primarily through oppressions but through anxieties and opportunities, not by constraint but by incitement and measurement and comparison. This happens in mundane ways, as we work on ourselves and others in conditions of 'well-regulated liberty' (Rose, 1999, p. 73).

More specifically, neo-liberalism is producing, as suggested previously, new kinds of social actors, hybrid social subjects who are spatially mobile, ethically malleable, and able to speak the languages of public, private and philanthropic value. Some of these are part of a global service class who are increasingly disconnected from national identities and loyalties (Ball, 2010a). However, Elliott and Lemert (2006) argue that the new freedoms of these cosmopolitan 'globals' is double-edged: 'The culture of advanced individualism has ushered into existence a world of individual risk-taking and experimentation and self-expression – which is in turn underpinned by new forms of apprehension, anguish and anxiety stemming from the perils of globalisation' (p. 12).

Together, these people, their relationships and interactions and morality and money and ideas and influence are transforming social, economic and political relations and enacting the neo-liberal imaginary in very real and practical ways in education and education policy. Neo-liberalism is insinuating itself into almost every aspect of contemporary social life.

This book is not comprehensive, in any sense, either substantively or analytically – many things are missing or have been treated superficially. I have tried to make my points through cases and exemplars. I have tried to open things up, point to possibilities, to things needing to be done, to tools that might be used, to ways of thinking about what is going on, about what is happening to us. However, the sense I end with is how much has not been done, how much more there is to map and trace and think about – before it is too late and other imaginaries are cast into the 'field of memory' or excluded from rational possibility.

Notes

1 At the time of writing I am still thinking about the analytic usefulness of assemblage. It is certainly useful in capturing the heterogeneity of social relations, the role of non-human actants and the fragility of these relations, but there is the danger that it is becoming another of those fashionable concepts that get widely but superficially used as a marker rather than a device – see Rizvi and Lingard (2011) for a good account.

References

Agranoff, R. (2003). A New look at the value-adding functions of intergovern-mental networks. Paper presented at the 7th National Public Management Research Conference, Georgetown University.

Amin, A. & Thrift, N. (2002). *Cities: Reimagining the Urban*. Cambridge: Polity Press.

Andersen, V. N., Dahler-Larsen, P. & Pedersen, C. S. (2009). Quality Assurance and evaluation in Denmark. *Journal of Education Policy, 24*(2), 135–47.

Appadurai, A. (1996). Global Ethnoscapes: Notes and Queries for a Transnational Anthropology. In R. G. Fox (Ed.), *Interventions: Anthropologies of the Present. Modernity at Large: Cultural Dimensions of Globalization*. Minneapolis: University of Minneapolis Press.

—— (2006). The right to research. *Globalisation, Societies and Education, 4*(2), 167–77.

Apple, M. (1995). *Education and Power* (2nd ed.). New York: Routledge.

Ball, S. J. (1994). *Education Reform: A Critical and Post-Structural Approach*. Buckingham: Open University Press.

—— (1997a). Markets, Equity and Values in Education. In R. Pring & G. Walford (eds), *Affirming the Comprehensive Ideal* (pp. 69–82). London: Falmer.

—— (1997b). 'On the Cusp': Parents Choosing between State and Private Schools. *International Journal of Inclusive Education, 1*(1), 1–17.

—— (2001a). Performativities and fabrications in the education economy: Towards the performative society. In D. Gleeson & C. Husbands (eds), *The Performing School: Managing teaching and learning in a performance culture*. London: Routledge-Falmer.

—— (2001b). Urban Choice and Urban Fears: The politics of parental choice. Paper presented at the Urban Education Symposium, Pädagogisches Institut der Stadt Wien, Vienna, Austria.

—— (2003a). *Class Strategies and the Education Market: the middle class and social advantage*. London: RoutledgeFalmer.

—— (2003b). The teacher's soul and the terrors of performativity. *Journal of Education Policy, 18*(2), 215–28.

—— (2007). *Education plc: Understanding private sector participation in public sector education*. London: Routledge.

—— (2008a). *The education debate: politics and policy in the 21st Century*. Bristol: Policy Press.

—— (2008b). The Legacy of ERA, Privatization and the Policy Ratchet. *Educational Management Administration and Leadership, 36*(2), 185–99.

—— (2009). Privatising education, privatising education policy, privatising educational research: network governance and the 'competition state'. *Journal of Education Policy, 42*(1), 83–99.

—— (2010a). Is there a global middle class? The beginnings of a cosmopolitan sociology of education: a review. *Journal of Comparative Education, 69*, 135–59.

—— (2010b). New Voices, New Knowledges and the New Politics of Education Research. *European Educational Research Journal, 9*(2), 124–37.

—— (2011a). Academies, policy networks and governance. In H. Gunter (Ed.), *The state and education policy: the academies programme.* London: Continuum.

—— (2011b). Global Education, Heterarchies, and Hybrid Organizations, in Ka-Ho MoK (Ed.), *The Search for New Governance of Higher Education in Asia.* Basingstoke, Palgrave Macmillian.

Ball, S. J., Bowe, R. and Gewirtz, S. (1996). School Choice, Social Class and Distinction: the realisation of social advantage in education. *Journal of Education Policy, 11*(1), 89–112.

Ball, S. J. & Junemann, C. (2012). *Networks, new governance and education.* Bristol: Policy Press.

Barber, M. (2007). *Instruction to Deliver: Tony Blair, the Public Services and the Challenge of Delivery.* London: Methuen.

Beck, U. (1992). *Risk Society: Towards a New Modernity.* Newbury Park, CA: Sage.

—— (2006). *Cosmopolitan Vision.* Cambridge: Polity Press.

Beck, U. & Grande, E. (2010). Varieties of second modernity: the cosmopolitan turn in social and political theory and research. *British Journal of Sociology, 61*(3), 409–43.

Bermingham, D. (2009). G8 in Italy Should Launch Global Fund for Education (Huffington Post), July 7, 2009, www.cgdev.org/content/article/detail/1422424

Besussi, E. (2006). Mapping European Research Networks. *Working Papers Series No. 103* Retrieved 7 August 2009, from Mapping European Research Networks.

Bevir, M. & Rhodes, R. A. W. (2006). *Governance Stories.* London: Routledge.

Blackmore, J. (1999). Localization/globalization and the midwife state: strategic dilemmas for state feminism in education? *Journal of Education Policy, 14*(1), 33–54.

Blaut, J. M. (1993). *The Colonizer's Model of the World: Geographical Diffusionism and Eurocentric History.* New York: Guildford Press.

Breeze, B. (2007). *More than Money: Why should sociologists be interested in philanthropy.* Paper presented at the British Sociological Association, UEL.

Brenner, N., Peck, J. & Theodore, N. (2010). Variegated neoliberalization: geographies, modalities, pathways. *Global Networks, 10*(1), 1.

Brenner, N. & Theodore, N. (2002). Cities and Geographies of 'Actually Existing Neoliberalism'. *Antipode, 34*(3), 351–79.

Brilliant, L., Wales, J. & Rodin, J. (2007). *The Changing Face of Philanthropy, Global Philanthropy.* Mountain View, CA: 6th Annual Conference, Financing Social Change: Leveraging markets and entrepreneurship.

Bronfman, C. & Solomon, J. (2009). *The Art of Giving: Where the Soul Meets a Business Plan.* New York: Jossey-Bass.

Brooks, S., Leach, M., Lucas, H. & Millstone, E. (2009). *Silver Bullets, Grand Challenges and the New Philanthropy*: STEPS Centre, University of Sussex.

Burch, P. E. (2006). The New Educational Privatization: Educational Contracting and High Stakes Accountability. *Teachers College Record, 108*(12), 2582–2610.

—— (2009). *Hidden Markets: The New Educational Privatization*. New York: Routledge.

Cavett-Goodwin, D. (2008). *Forces Constructing Consent for the Neoliberal Project*. Retrieved 24 Match 2009, from culturalshifts.com/archives/206.

Cerny, P. (1997). Paradoxes of the competition state: The dynamics of political globalisation. *Government and Opposition, 32*(2), 251–74.

Choudaha, R. (2001). Drivers of mobility of Chinese and Indian students. *International Higher Education, 62*, 26–28.

Clarke, J. (2008). Living with/in and without neo-liberalism. *Focaal – European Journal of Anthropology, 51*(1), 135–47.

Clarke, J. & Newman, J. (1997). *The Mangerial State*. London: Sage.

Cohen, N. (2004). *Pretty Straight Guys*. London: Faber and Faber.

Cole, D. R. (Ed.). (2012). *Surviving economic crises through education*. Peter Lang.

Connell, R., Fawcett, B. & Meagher, G. (2009). Neoliberalism, New Public Management and the human service professions: Introduction to the Special Issue. *Journal of Sociology, 45*(4), 331–38.

Coulson, A. J. (2007). An invisible hand up: the Orient Global Education Fund aims to show how for-profit schools can work in the developing world. *Philanthropy Magazine*, Philanthropy Roundtable, 6 August 2007. Available at http://www.philanthropyroundtable.org/article.asp?article=1479&cat=139.

Dale, R. (2006). From comparison to translation: extending the research imagination? *Globalisation, Societies and Education, 4*(2), 179–92.

Dalton, R. J. & Rohrschneider, R. (2003). The Environmental Movement and the Modes of Political Action. *Comparative Political Studies, 36*(7), 743–71.

Davies, D. (2005). The (Im)possibility of Intellectual Work in Neoliberal Regimes, *Discourse* 2(6), 1–14.

Davies, J. S. (2005). Local Governance and the Dialectics of Hierarchy, Market and Network. *Policy Studies, 26*(3/4), 311–35.

Derrida, J. (1996). Remarks on deconstruction and pragmatism, in C. Mouffe (Ed.), *Deconstruction and Pragmatism*, pp. 77–88, London: Routledge.

Dezalay, Y. & Garth, B. G. (2002). *The Internationalization of Palace Wars: Lawyers, Economists and the contest to transform Latin-American States*. Chicago: University of Chicago Press.

Dicken, P., Kelly, P. F. & Yeung, H. W. C. (2001). Chains and Networks, territories and scales: towards a relational framework for analysing the global economy. *Global Networks, 1*(1), 89–112.

Doherty, B. (2007). *Radicals for capitalism: a freewheeling history of the modern American libertarian movement*. New York: Public Affairs.

Dolowitz, D. & Marsh, D. (2000). Learning from abroad: the role of policy transfer in contemporary policy making. *Governance, 13*(1), 5–24.

Edwards, M. (2008). *Just Another Emperor? The Myths and Realities of Philanthrocapitalism*. London: Demos and The Young Foundation.

Elliott, A. & Lemert, C. (2006). *The New Individualism: The Emotional Costs of Globalisation*. Abingdon: Routledge.

Elmore, R. F. (2009). *Building a New Structure For School Leadership*. http://www.ashankerinst.org/Downloads/building.pdf.

Falk, C. (1999). Sentencing Learners to Life: Retrofitting the Academy for the Information Age. *Theory, Technology and Culture, 22*(1–2), 19–27.

Fazackerley, A. E. (2007). *British Universities in China: The Reality Beyond the Rhetoric*. London Agora: a forum for culture and education.

Florini, A. (Ed.). (2000). *The Third Force: The Rise of Transnational Civil Society*. Tokyo: Japan Centre for International Exchange.

Foucault, M. (1979). *Discipline and Punish*. Harmondsworth: Peregrine.

—— (2004). *Society Must be Defended*. London: Penguin Books.

Frumkin, P. (2006). *Strategic Giving: The Art and Science of Philanthropy*. Chicago: The University of Chicago Press.

Fullan, M. G. (2001). *Leading in a Culture of Change*. San Fransisco: Jossey Bass.

Goodwin, M. (2009). Which Networks Matter in Educational Governance? A Reply to Ball's 'New Philanthropy, New Networks and New Governance in Education'. *Political Studies, 57*(3), 608–87.

Grabher, G. (2004). Learning in projects, remembering in networks? Communality, sociality, and connectivity in project ecologies. *European Urban and Regional Studies, 11*(2), 103–23.

Graefe, P. (2005). Roll-out Neoliberalism and the Social Economy. Paper presented at the Canadian Political Science Association.

Grek, S., Lawn, M., Lingard, B. & Varjo, J. (2009). North by northwest: quality assurance and evaluation processes in European education. *Journal of Education Policy, 24*(2), 121–33.

Grek, S. & Ozga, J. (2010). Re-Inventing Public Education: The New Role of Knowledge in Education Policy Making. *Public Policy and Administration, 25*(2), 271–88.

Gunter, H. (2010). School Leadership and educational policymaking in England. *Policy Studies*.

Gunter, H. M., & Forrester, G. (2010). School Leadership and Policymaking in England. *Policy Studies, 31*(1), 495–511.

Hannam, K., Sheller, M. & Urry, J. (2006). Mobilities, immobilities and moorings. *Mobilities, 1*(1), 1–22.

Harrison, S. & Wood, B. (1999). Designing Health Service Organisation in the UK, 1968–98: From Blueprint to Bright Idea and 'Manipulated Emergence'. *Public Administration, 77*(4), 751–68.

Harvey, D. (2005). *A Brief History of Neo-Liberalism*. Oxford: Oxford University Press.

Hayek, F. (1944). *The Road to Serfdom*. London: George Routledge & Sons.

Held, D. & McGrew. (2004). The Great Globalization Debate: An Introduction. In Held & McGrew (eds), *The Global Transformations Reader: An Introduction to the Globalization Debate*. Oxford: Polity.

Holden, C. (2009). Exporting Public-Private Partnerships in Healthcare: Export Strategy and Policy Transfer. *Policy Studies, 30*(3), 313–32.

Horne, J. R. (2002). *A Social Laboratory for Modern France: The Musée Social and the Rise of the Welfare State*. New York: Sage.

Howard, P. N. (2002). Network Ethnography and the Hypermedia Organization: New Media, New Organizations, New Methods. *New Media and Society, 4*(4), 550–74.

Hunter, I. (1996). Assembling the School. In A. Barry, T. Osborne & N. Rose (eds), *Foucault and Political Reason: Liberalism, Neo-liberalism and Rationalities of Government*. London: UCL Press.

Jackson, J. M. & Bassett, E. (2005). *The state of the K-12 state assessment market*. Boston: Eduventures.

Jessop, B. (1997). The Entrepreneurial City: re-imagining localities, redesigning economic governance, or restructuring capital? In N. Jewson & S. Macgregor (eds), *Transforming Cities: contested governance and spatial dimensions*. London: Routledge.

—— (1998). The Rise of Governance and the risks of failure. *International Social Science Journal, 155*(1), 29–45.

—— (2002). *The Future of the Capitalist State.* Cambridge: Polity.

Jessop, B., Brenner, N. & Jones, M. (2008). Theorizing sociospatial relations. *Environment and Planning D; Society and Space, 26,* 389–401.

John, P. (2003). Is there life after policy streams, advocacy coalitions, and punctuations?: using evolutionary theory to explain policy change. *Policy Studies, 31*(4), 481–98.

Jones, K. (2010). Crisis, what crisis? *Journal of Education Policy, 25*(6), 793–98.

Kamat, S. (2011). Neoliberalism, Cities and Education in the Global South/North. *Discourse: Studies in the Cultural Politics of Education, 32*(2), 187–202.

Keck, M. E. & Sikkink, K. (1998). *Activists Beyond Borders: Advocacy Networks in International Politics.* Ithaca: Cornell University Press.

Kelsey, J. (2006). Taking minds to market. Retrieved from http://www.knowpol. uib.no/portal/files/uplink/kelsey.pdf.

Kingdon, J. W. (1995). *Agendas, alternatives, and public policies.* New York: Harper-Collins.

Kooiman, J. (Ed.). (1993). *Modern governance: new government–society interactions.* London: Sage.

Kovacs, P. E. (Ed.). (2010). *The Gates Foundation and the Future of US 'Public' Schools.* London: Routledge.

LaDousa, C. (2007). Liberalisation, privatisation, modernisation and schooling in India: an interview with Krishna Kumar. *Globalisation, Societies and Education, 5*(2), 137–52.

Larbi, G. A. (1999). *The New Public Management Approach and Crisis States (Vol. Discussion Paper No. 112).* United Nations Research Institute for Social Development.

Larner, W. (2002). Globalization, governmentality and expertise: creating a call centre labour force. *Review of International Political Economy, 9*(4), 650–74.

—— (2003). Neoliberalism? *Environment and Planning D: Society and Space, 21,* 509–12.

Larner, W. & Le Heron, R. (2002). The spaces and subjects of a globalizing economy: a situated exploration of method. *Environment and Planning D: Society and Space, 20,* 753–74.

Lingard, B. (2009). Testing Times: The need for new intelligent accountabilities for schooling. *QTU Professional Magazine.* Retrieved from http://www.qtu.asn.au/ vo24_lingard.pdf.

Lyotard, J. F. (1984). *The Postmodern Condition: A Report on Knowledge* (Vol. 10). Manchester: Manchester University Press.

Mackenzie, R. & Lucio, M. M. (2005). The Realities of Regulatory Change: Beyond the Fetish of Deregulation. *British Journal of Sociology, 39*(3), 499–517.

Mahony, P., Menter, I. & Hextall, I. (2004). Building Dams in Jordan, assessing teachers in England: a case study in edu-business. *Globalisation, Societies and Education, 2*(2), 277–96.

March, J. G. & Olsen, J. P. (1989). *Rediscovering institutions: the organisational basis of politics.* New York: Free Press.

Marcus, G. & Saka, E. (2006). Assemblage. *Theory, Culture and Society, 23*(2/3), 101–7.

Marginson, S. (2006). Notes on globalization and higher education: With some reference to the case of Australia. Clayton, Vic.: Monash Centre for Research in International Education, Monash University.

Marginson, S. & Sawir, E. (2005). Interrogating global flows in higher education. *Globalization, Societies and Education, 3*(3), 281–310.

Marin, B. & Mayntz, R. (eds). (1991). *Policy networks: empirical evidence and theoretical considerations*. Frankfurt am Main, Boulder, Colorado, Campus Verlag: Westview.

Marsh, D. & Smith, M. (2000). Understanding policy networks: towards a dialectical approach. *Political Studies, 48*, 4–21.

Martens, K. & Starke, P. (2008). Small Country, Big Business? New Zealand as an Education Exporter. *Comparative Education, 44*(1), 3–19.

McCann, E. J. (2011). Urban policy mobilities and global circuits of knowledge. *Annals of Association of American Geographers, 101*(1), 107–130.

McCowan, T. (2004). The Growth of Private Higher Education in Brazil: Implications for Equity and Quality. *Journal of Education Policy, 19*(4), 453–72.

Mintrom, M. & Vergari, S. (1996). Advocacy Coalitions, Policy Entrepreneurs, and Policy Change. *Policy Studies Journal, 24*(3), 420–34.

Mok, K. H. (2007). Globalisation, new education governance and state capacity in East Asia. *Globalisation, Societies and Education, 5*(1), 1–21.

Nambissan, G. B. & Ball, S. J. (2010). Advocacy networks, choice and private schooling of the poor in India. *Global Networks, 10*(3), 1–20.

Newman, J. (2001). *Modernising Governance: New Labour, Policy and Society*. London: Sage.

Oborn, E., Barrett, M. & Exworthy, M. (2011). Policy entrepreneurship in the development of public sector strategy: the case of London health reform. *Public Administration, 89*(2), 325–44.

Olssen, M., Codd, J. & O'Neill, A. M. (2004). *Education Policy: Globalization, citizenship, democracy*. London: Sage.

Ong, A. (2006). Mutations in Citizenship. *Theory, Culture and Society, 23*(2–3), 499–505.

—— (2007). Neoliberalism as a mobile technology. *Transactions of the Institute of British Geographers, 32*(1), 3–8.

Osborne, D. & Gaebler, T. (1992). *Re-inventing Government*. Reading, Mass.: Addison-Wesley.

Ozga, J. (2008). Governing Knowledge: research steering and research quality. *European Educational Research Journal, 7*(3), 261–72.

—— (2009). Governing education through data in England: from regulation to self-evaluation. *Special Issue of Journal of Education Policy, 24*(2), 149–63.

Parker, R. (2007). Networked Governance or Just Networks? Local Governance of the Knowledge Economy in Limerick (Ireland) and Karlskrona (Sweden). *Political Studies, 55*(1), 113–32.

Peck, J. (2003). Geography and public policy: mapping the penal state. *Progress in Human Geography, 27*(2), 222–32.

—— (2010). Neoliberal Worlds. *Oxford Scholarship Online Monographs*.

Peck, J. & Tickell, A. (2002). Neoliberalizing Space. *Antipode, 34*(3), 380–404.

—— (2003). Making global rules: globalisation or neoliberalisation? In J. Peck & H. Yeung (eds), *Remaking the Global Economy*. London: Sage.

Peet, R. (2000). Geographies of Policy Formation: Hegemony, Discourse and the Conquest for Practicality. Paper presented at the Geographies of Global Economic Change.

Peterson, J. (2003). *Policy Networks*. Vienna: Institute for Advanced Studies.

Pierre, J. (Ed.). (2000). *Debating Governance*. Oxford: Oxford University Press.

Pierre, J. & Peters, B. G. (2000). *Governance, Politics, and the State*. Basingstoke: Macmillan Press.

Power, M. (1994). *The Audit Explosion*. London: Demos.

Rhodes, R. A. W. (1997). *Understanding Governance: Policy Networks, Governance, Reflexivity and Accountability*. Buckingham: Open University Press.

Richards, D. & Smith, M. J. (2002). *Governance and Public Policy in the United Kingdom*. Oxford: Oxford University Press.

Riles, A. (2000). *The Network Inside Out*. Ann Arbor: University of Michigan Press.

Rinne, R., Kallo, J. & Hokka, S. (2004). Too Eager to Comply? OECD Education Policies and the Finnish Response. *European Educational Research Journal, 2*(2), 454–85.

Rinne, R., Kivirauma, J. & Simola, H. (2002). Shoots of revisionist education policy or just slow readjustment? The Finnish case of educational reconstruction. *Journal of Education Policy, 17*(6), 643–58.

Rizvi, F. & Lingard, B. (2010). *Globalizing Education Policy*. London: Routledge.

—— (2011). Social equity and the assemblage of values in Australian higher education. *Cambridge Journal of Education, 41*(1), 5–22.

Rose, N. (1996). Governing 'advanced' liberal democracies. In A. Barry, T. Osborne & N. Rose (eds), *Foucault and Political Reason: Liberalism, neo-liberalism and rationalities of government*. London: UCL Press.

—— (1999). *Powers of Freedom: Reframing Political Thought*. Cambridge: Cambridge University Press.

—— (2007). *Psychology as Social Science*. Retrieved 2 June, 2010.

Saltman, K. J. (2005). *The Edison Schools: Corporate Schooling and the Assault on Public Education*. New York: Routledge.

—— (2007). *Capitalizing on Disaster: Taking and Breaking Public Schools*. New York: Paradigm Publishers.

—— (2010). *The Gift of Education: Public Education and Venture Philanthropy*. New York: Palgrave-Macmillan.

Scharpf, F. W. (1994). Games real actors could play: positive and negative coordination in embedded organisations. *Journal of Theoretical Politics, 6*(1), 27–53.

Shamir, R. (2008). The age of responsibilitization: on market-embedded morality. *Economy and Society, 37*(1), 1–19.

Shore, C. & Wright, S. (1999). Audit Culture and Anthropology: Neo-liberalism in British Higher Education. *The Journal of the Royal Anthropological Institute, 5*(4), 557–75.

Skelcher, C. (1998). *The Appointed State*. Buckingham: Open University Press.

Slaughter, S. & Leslie, L. (1997). *Academic Capitalism: Politics, Policies and the Entrepreneurial University*. Boston: Johns Hopkins University Press.

Sorenson, E. & Tofting, J. (eds). (2007). *Theories of Democratic Network Governance*. Basingstoke: Palgrave-Macmillan.

Spring, J. (2008). Research on Globalization and Education. *Review of Educational Research, 78*(2), 330–63.

Stewart, R., van Rooyen, C., Dickson, K., Majoro, M. & de Wet, T. (2011). *What is the Impact of Microfinance on Poor People? A systematic review of evidence from Sub-Saharan Africa*. London: EPPI-Centre, Social Science Research Unit, Institute of Education.

Stone, D. (1999). Learning lessons and transferring policy across time, space and disciplines. *Politics, 19*(1), 51–59.

—— (2000). Private Authority, scholarly legitimacy and political credibility: think tanks and informal diplomacy. In R. A. Higgott, G. R. D. Underhill & A. Biler (eds), *Non-State Actors and Authority in the Global System*. London: Routledge.

—— (2004). Transfer agents and global networks in the 'transnationalization' of policy. *Journal of European Public Policy, 11*(3), 545–66.

—— (2008). *The new networks of knowledge: think tanks and the transnationalization of governance*. New York: Social Science Research Council.

Tabb, W. (2002). *Unequal Partners: a primer in globalization*. New York: The New Press.

Thrift, N. (2005). *Knowing Capitalism*. London: Sage.

Tooley, J. (1999). *The Global Education Industry*. London: Institute of Economic Affairs.

—— (2009). *The Beautiful Tree*. Washington, DC: Cato Institute.

Tuschling, A. & Engemann, C. (2006). From Education to Lifelong Learning: The emerging regime of learning in the European Union. *Educational Philosophy and Theory, 38*(4), 451–69.

UNESCO. (2011). *The Hidden Crisis: Armed Conflict and Education*. Paris: UNESCO.

Urry, J. (2003). Social networks, travel and talk. *British Journal of Sociology, 54*(2), 155–75.

—— (2004). Small Worlds and the New 'Social Physics'. *Global Networks, 4*(2), 109–30.

Vander Ark, T. (2009). *Private Capital and Public Education: Toward Quality at Scale*. Washington: American Institute for Enterprise and Public Policy.

Wacquant, L. (1999). How Penal Common Sense Comes to Europeans: Notes on the Transatlantic Diffusion of Neoliberal Doxa. *European Societies, 1*(3), 319–52.

Wapner, P. (1996). *Environmental Activism and World Civic Politics*. Albany: SUNY.

Whitehead, M. (2003). 'In the shadow of hierarchy': meta-governance, policy reform and urban regeneration in the West Midlands. *AREA, 35*(1), 6–14.

Williams, P. (2002). The competent boundary spanner. *Public Administration, 80*(1), 103–24.

Wolch, J. (1990). *The shadow state: government and voluntary sector in transition*. New York: The Foundation Center.

Yang, R., Vidovich, L. & Currie, J. (2007). University accountability practices in mainland China and Hong Kong: A comparative analysis. *Asian Journal of University Education, 2*(1), 1–21.

Yeatman, A. (1996). The New Contractualism: Management Reform or a New Approach to Governance? In G. Davis & P. Weller (eds), *New Ideas, Better Government*. St Leonards, Australia: Allen and Unwin.

Index

Please note that page numbers relating to Notes will have the letter 'n' following the page number. References to Figures or Tables will be in *italic* print.